S T U D Y ⊗ G U I D E

THE BONDAGE BREAKER

YOUTH EDITION

Neil T. Anderson & Dave Park

HARVEST HOUSE PUBLISHERS
Eugene, Oregon 97402

Cover by Terry Dugan Design, Minneapolis, Minnesota

The names of certain individuals mentioned in this book have been changed in order to protect their privacy.

THE BONDAGE BREAKER YOUTH EDITION STUDY GUIDE
Copyright © 1995, 2001 by Harvest House Publishers
Published by Harvest House Publishers
Eugene, Oregon 97402

ISBN 0-7369-0627-4

Printed in the United States of America.

01 02 03 04 05 06 07 08 09 10 / BP-MS / 10 9 8 7 6 5 4 3 2 1

Contents

In Christ

One of the best ways to know God better is to get into His Word, the Bible. And reading Christian books and study guides like this one is a great way to strengthen your walk with Him.

Before you begin each lesson, take time to pray and ask God to teach you new truths about Him. Ephesians 1:18-21 says, "I pray that the eyes of your heart may be enlightened, so that you will know what is the hope of His calling, what are the riches of the glory of His inheritance in the saints, and what is the surpassing greatness of His power toward us who believe. These are in accordance with the working of the strength of His might which He brought about in Christ, when He raised Him from the dead and seated Him at His right hand in the heavenly places, far above all rule and authority and power and dominion, and every name that is named, not only in this age but also in the one to come."

Like Paul the apostle, we (Neil and Dave) are praying that as you study God's Word, the eyes of your heart will be open to the hope of your calling, your inheritance, and your authority in Christ. And remember—you are not just studying *The Bondage Breaker Youth Edition Study Guide*, but *Jesus*, who is your Bondage Breaker.

Part 1

Take Courage!

You Don't Have to Live in the Shadows

Are You Living in the Shadows?

> Dear God,
>
> Where are you? How can you watch and not help me? I hurt so bad, and you don't even care. If you cared, you'd make it stop or let me die. I love you, but you seem so far away. I can't hear you or feel you or see you, but I'm supposed to believe you're here....

You may have asked these very questions and felt some of these feelings yourself. The woman who wrote these words before she unsuccessfully tried to commit suicide may be voicing pain that you've felt. If so, know that the message of this chapter—and this book—is that you don't have to live in the shadows created by such dark thoughts.

- Your darkness may not involve voices in your head. Many young Christians don't complain about hearing voices, but they will say that their daily walk with Christ is really discouraging. When they try to pray, they begin thinking about the million things they should be doing. When they sit down to read the Bible or a book by a Christian author, they can't concentrate. When they have an opportunity to serve the Lord, they are overwhelmed by self-doubt ("I'm not a strong enough Christian"; "I don't know enough about the Bible"), so they don't even try.

— Which of these struggles do you face? Where, if at all, are you discouraged in your Christian walk?

— The kind of discouragement described above can come from our own faulty thinking, but it can also be a sign that the enemy is attacking. How might the enemy be deceiving you right now? In what area of your life might he be trying to keep you from growing?

Whether or not you are hearing voices in your head (and many of the young people we surveyed do), you need to know how to defend yourself against Satan's fiery darts, whatever shape they come in. So keep reading.

Common Misconceptions about Bondage

• First, what do you think about when you hear the word "bondage"? What do you feel when you hear that word?

• The evil voices, guilty feelings, and confusion you read about in *The Bondage Breaker Youth Edition* are ways that Satan can keep us in bondage. And one reason he is able to do so is because we don't understand the spiritual world. Review pages 21–26 in the text, which is the discussion of the misconceptions listed below.

1. *Demons were busy when Christ was on earth, but they're not around much today.*

   — What does Paul's warning in Ephesians 6:12-18 suggest about how busy demons are or aren't today?

   — What evidence do you see of demon activity today?

2. *What early Christians called demonic activity is only mental illness.*

   — Why would many psychologists never bring up the possibility of demonic activity?

   — Why is Satan the deceiver pleased with this fact?

3. *Some problems are psychological and some are spiritual.*

   — Why can't we draw a line like this between our psyche (our mind) and our spirit?

   — When have you personally been aware of the indivisible connection between your heart, your mind, your spirit, and your body?

4. *Christians can't be attacked by demonic forces.*

— Again, what does Paul's warning in Ephesians 6:12-18 say that proves the statement above is wrong?

— And, again, why is Satan the deceiver pleased with the popularity of this misconception?

5. *The activity of demons is only seen in weird behavior or gross sin.*

— How does Satan benefit from this misunderstanding of his activity?

— What does Paul's teaching in 2 Corinthians 11:14,15 suggest about the shape of demon influence?

6. *Freedom from spiritual bondage is the result of a power encounter with demonic forces.*

— What does Neil's boyhood experience with the farm dog teach you about Satan's activity?

— What is significant to you about the fact that a truth encounter—not a power encounter—is what leads to freedom from spiritual bondage?

• Which of the misconceptions listed above have you encoun-
  tered? If you have accepted any of them as true, how has
  doing so affected your life?

• Take time to read God's truth. What do the following verses
  say about Satan and Christ?
    — John 8:44

    — John 10:10

    — John 14:6

• What have you learned so far about the reality of the spiritual
  world? In three or four sentences, sum up what the Bible
  teaches about the spiritual world.

Satan deceives us. His power is in the lie: He wants you and me to
believe and live a lie. As a Christian, however, you have the power
that comes with knowing the truth. When you believe, declare,
and act on the truth you find in God's Word, you ruin Satan's
strategy and find freedom.

Setting Captives Free

Something radical happened at the cross and in the resurrection that permanently changed the way we encounter spiritual forces.

- First, in His death and resurrection, Jesus defeated and disarmed the rulers of darkness (Colossians 2:15) and was given all authority "in heaven and on earth" (Matthew 28:18). Because of the cross, Satan is defeated; he has no authority over those who are in Christ. Second, in Christ's death and resurrection, every believer is made alive with Him and lives in Him.

  — What do these truths say about how you can respond when Satan harasses you?

  — The next time you're feeling hassled by Satan, how will you respond? What will you do to exercise your position and authority in Christ? Be specific.

  — If you want to learn more about standing strong against Satan, to whom will you go for help?

- Since you are in Christ, you never again need to live in the shadows. Instead, from your position in Christ, you are responsible for choosing the truth and resisting the devil. You are responsible for renouncing (turning your back on) the ways you have participated in his schemes. (We'll discuss this in greater detail in Part Three.)

  — At this point, what behaviors do you need to confess as wrong and stop doing?

— What attitudes (pride, hard-heartedness, envy, and so on) do you need to renounce and release?

— And to whom do you need to extend forgiveness?

We are able to choose the truth and resist the devil because of who we are in Christ. Fully understanding God's provision for you in Christ is key to understanding how He can be your Bondage Breaker.

- "A Lost Sheep" came to a better understanding of who she is in Christ. Turn to page 28 of the text and read again the letter she wrote in response to her own earlier cry for help.

  — Which words of truth do you especially need to hear right now? Write them out below and know that they are indeed God's words to you.

  — What words of hope from this letter do you want to believe with your heart as well as your head? Ask God to help you believe.

The truth of who you are in Jesus Christ is the light that can and will dispel the shadows in your life.

A Step Toward Freedom

Here and throughout the study guide, you'll have a chance to take *A Step Toward Freedom*. Since freedom comes from Jesus, the Bondage Breaker, and His truth, the steps will involve Scripture and prayer.

- Which of the following verses is an especially effective reminder of the truth that God's love and power in Christ is what frees us from Satan's grip? Write out the verse you choose on an index card and memorize it.

    –John 14:6

    –John 17:15,17

    –Philippians 4:8

    –Romans 8:38,39

    –1 Peter 3:21b,22

- Spend a few minutes in prayer and ask God to help you recognize any misunderstanding you might have about Him, Satan, and the spiritual world. Then ask the Lord to replace those misconceptions with His truth. You might also ask Him to provide a more mature believer (such as a pastor or youth leader) who can help guide you to a better understanding of God's truth.

Also, if you are feeling as if you could have written the letter by "A Lost Sheep," find someone trustworthy you can share your feelings with and have that person pray with you and for you during these dark days. Finally, ask God to help you grow in your understanding of who you are in Christ.

Finding Your Way in the World

TWO

Have You Been Caught in Satan's Web?

• In his novel *Lord of the Flies*, what does William Golding propose as the source of evil in the world? Why does Satan not interfere with this idea?

• What does Dave's description of the chicken he found waiting for him after his three-week trip suggest to you about Satan's strategy in the world?

• Perhaps you have unknowingly entered into Satan's realm. Today's popular culture innocently offers many avenues. Which of the following, if any, have you "played with" or enjoyed but never taken seriously?

    Dungeons & Dragons

    Ouija boards

    Movies like *Mummy, The Sixth Sense, The Exorcist*

15

Palm-reading

New Age ideas (channeling, spirit guides)

Satan—the one who lures people into his trap through parapsychology, our culture's fascination with the supernatural, and the popularizing of Ouija boards, astrology, Dungeons & Dragons, and palm-reading—would like us to believe that he doesn't really exist and that evil is just a human weakness.

The Two-Level Worldview

The word "worldview" refers to how you understand the world around you, how you relate to it, and what you believe about reality. But neither the two-level Western worldview nor the Eastern worldview (both described in the text on pages 33–35) reflects the truth of the Bible.

- Missions expert Dr. Paul Hiebert points to something between the seen world of the senses and the unseen world of God and spiritual forces and calls it the "excluded middle." What happens in this excluded middle, which is excluded from our minds only because we choose to ignore it?

- Remember Dee? She learned that the real world includes spiritual forces that are active in the seen, physical world. What did you learn from Dee's experience?

- Do you, like Dee's father, tend not to consider the possibility of spiritual causes for physical ailments? What can result from not considering the possible spiritual root of physical problems?

When we exclude the supernatural from our worldview or believe it has no effect on our lives, we exclude God's power from our beliefs and practices. We also tend to explain all human problems as resulting from mental or physical causes rather than spiritual ones.

Living in the Excluded Middle

- Scripture clearly teaches that supernatural forces are at work in the world. What do the following passages teach about those forces?

  — Mark 5:1-20

  — Luke 13:11-13

  — Ephesians 6:12

- Neil and Dave encourage you to see both your doctor, who will test and treat you physically, *and* your pastor, who should be able to test and treat you spiritually. Why is this balanced approach reasonable and important?

Getting Spiritual Without God

Unsatisfied by the materialistic world as well as unhappy with organized religion, many young people today turn to the occult,

Eastern religions, and New Age ideas to try to fill their spiritual emptiness. In other words, they try to get spiritual without God.

- When God is not at the center of our lives, who steps in?

- When we become our own god, what happens to our primary concerns?

- In Matthew 16:13-23, how does the apostle Peter illustrate the struggle between living for self and living for Christ?

- In what areas of your life do you especially struggle with living for Christ instead of for yourself?

Satan's primary aim is to get us to center our lives on our own interests—"Save yourself at all costs! Watch out for yourself! Don't do anything that is painful or inconvenient!" But the Christian looks at life from a different perspective: Ours is the view from the cross.

The View from the Cross

This view shatters Satan's lie that we human beings can be our own gods. We were not designed to be gods, and we never will be gods. We must replace the false idea that we can be gods (popularized in this generation by the New Age movement) with the teachings of Jesus. The following six guidelines, based on Jesus' words in Matthew 16:24-27, will free you from the bondage of the world system and the devil who inspires it. These guidelines will help you find your way in a dark world.

Deny Yourself

- Explain how denying yourself is not the same as self-denial. Consider, for starters, the ultimate purpose of each.

- Why is denying yourself essential to spiritual freedom?

Pick Up Your Cross Daily

- What has the cross of Christ provided for believers? See, for instance, John 3:16 and 2 Corinthians 5:21.

- What does the phrase "pick up your cross" mean? Be specific— and remember that the cross we're referring to is Christ's cross.

Follow Christ

- Where will the path of following Christ lead you? Does that destination sound good? Why or why not?

- Only when you have come to the end of your own resources (died to self-rule) will you discover God's resources. What will such an experience teach you? What will you gain?

The instruction to deny yourself, pick up your cross daily, and follow Christ may sound as if you are sacrificing yourself and gaining nothing. But consider now what you're sacrificing and what you're gaining.

Sacrifice the Lower Life to Gain the Higher Life

- How are you trying to save your natural life? Are you trying to find your identity and sense of worth in positions, titles, grades, friends, accomplishments, or possessions? How is pursuing these things interfering with your pursuit of spiritual things?

- If you shoot for this world, that's all you'll get—and eventually you'll lose even that. But if you shoot for the next world, God will throw this one in as a bonus (1 Timothy 4:8). What can you do to shoot for the next world instead of this one? Be specific.

Sacrifice the Pleasure of Things to Gain the Pleasure of Life

- Identify two or three ways the world says that fame and possessions will bring you love, joy, peace, and patience—that is, the fruit of God's Spirit (Galatians 5:22,23). Which worldly pleasures have you looked to for love, joy, peace, and patience?

• Read Luke 10:38-42. What was Martha interested in? What was Mary interested in? Are you more like Martha, loving things, or Mary, loving God and people? Support your answer with specific evidence from your life.

Sacrifice the Temporary to Gain the Eternal

• Look again at Hebrews 11:24-26. What did Moses sacrifice? What did he hope to gain by doing so?

• What temporary things are you sacrificing—or could you sacrifice—to gain the eternal rewards of heaven?

Whenever you live independently of God, focusing on yourself instead of Christ, seeking material and worldly things over spiritual and eternal things, Satan couldn't be more pleased. After all, he wants to take God's place in your life by convincing you that you can be your own God.

A Step Toward Freedom

- Read Matthew 16:24-27 again.
- What are some practical ways you can pick up your cross daily and follow Jesus?

- Why do we have so much trouble denying ourselves and following Christ? What role can prayer play in enabling us to pick up the cross each day and follow Jesus?

- Ask God to show you what He would have you do to deny yourself...pick up your cross...and follow Him more closely. Ask Him to give you a deeper longing for the higher life rather than the lower life...greater desire for the pleasure of life in Him rather than pleasure in worldly things...and greater hunger for eternal things rather than the temporary things of the world. Then close your prayer by asking Him to teach you how to live each moment in "Christ, who is our life" (Colossians 3:4).

You Have Every Right to Be Free

THREE

A Dearly Loved Child of God

- Answer the two questions Neil asked Lydia: "Who are you?" and "How do you see yourself?"

- Satan had deceived Lydia into believing she was worthless and evil. Has he deceived you or do your answers above reflect a solid understanding of who you are in Christ?

- Turn to the "Who Am I?" list on pages 45–48 in the text and read it again. Think of some reasons that Satan doesn't want us to know and believe these truths.

- How had not knowing and believing the truth affected Lydia's life?

Nothing is more basic to our freedom from Satan's bondage than understanding what God has done for us in Christ and who we are as a result. If you see yourself as the dearly loved and accepted child of God that you really are, your attitudes, actions, and responses to life's circumstances will be very different than if you see yourself as evil and worthless. In this chapter, we'll look closely at who we are in Christ. Believe these words of truth! They are for you!

You Are a Child of God

- Turn in your Bible to 1 John 3:1-3. What is our relationship to God the Father, based on what He has done? What is our hope now?

- Think again about being a child of God. How will believing this about yourself affect your life?

You Are Spiritually and Therefore Eternally Alive

When we were born again, our soul/spirit was united with God and we came alive spiritually. And this spiritual life we have received in Christ is eternal.

- Read Ephesians 1:1-14, noticing especially verses 7 and 13. What is your standing in relation to Christ once you accept Him as your Savior and Lord?

- What promise, quoted in Hebrews 13:5, guarantees the security of the eternal life you have in Christ?

- What causes you to doubt your relationship with Christ? With what truth in the Bible can you answer and dispel that idea, which comes straight from Satan himself?

You Are Changed
from Sinner to Saint

Christians who consider themselves "just sinners saved by grace" tend to be defeated Christians rather than victorious, effective believers.

- Do you see yourself as a sinner or a saint? Explain.

- Why does seeing ourselves as sinners—even sinners saved by grace—often lead to despair and more sinning?

- How can seeing yourself as a saint—who sometimes sins—
  help you stand strong against sin and Satan? What specific
  truths from the Bible can also help you?

You Have Been Given God's Divine Nature

Ephesians 2:1-3 describes our nature before we came to Christ:
Our nature was sin, and the result of our sin was death (separa-
tion from God). But at salvation God changed us: We received His
divine nature (2 Peter 1:4; 2 Corinthians 5:17; Ephesians 5:8).

- How have your thoughts, words, and actions changed since
  you became a Christian? How does your behavior reflect the
  fact that you are a new creature in Christ (2 Corinthians 5:17)?

- Being a new creation in Christ doesn't mean being sinless.
  What sins do you battle? Where are you choosing to act independently of God?

- How does the fact that you are a partaker of God's divine
  nature encourage you in your walk of faith, despite your sins?

- Look over the list of the ways in which you are identified with
  Christ (on page 52 in the text). What does it mean to you to
  be "in Him" in each of these areas?

You Can Be Victorious over the Flesh and Sin

When our old sinful self died, sin's rule as our master ended. But sin is still around. Even though sin's power and authority have been broken (Romans 8:2), sin remains strong and appealing. It is our responsibility not to let sin rule in our body.

- Look again at Romans 6:12,13. What is God commanding you specifically?

- What peer pressure do you feel to serve sin rather than God with your body? Confess where you have chosen to serve sin.

- What are you doing—or could you be doing—to stand strong against the appeal of sin and the apparent popularity of certain sinful actions? One thing you could be doing is asking God to give you the strength you need to live out what you know is true.

You Can Be Free from the Power of Sin

In Romans 7:15-25, Paul shares the frustrations that come with battling sin and points to God's path to freedom from the power of sin.

- Walk slowly through Dan and Neil's dialogue about this passage on pages 55–60 of the text.

— Romans 7:15-17. (How many players are there? Identify them.)

— Romans 7:18-21. (Which player is bad? Why is that good news for Dan and you?)

— Romans 7:22-25. (Where does the battle rage? What is causing the pain? Who is the source of victory?)

• How do you respond to your own sinfulness? Do you condemn yourself rather than confessing and submitting to God and resisting the devil?

• Where do you most identify with Dan (and the apostle Paul)?

• What hope did the apostle Paul find in his struggle with sin? What words from Dan and Neil's discussion offer you new insight and hope?

A Step Toward Freedom

- Look again at pages ms 45-48 in the text, which list the Bible's answers to the question, Who am I? Choose one or two passages to memorize as reminders of who you are in Christ.

- Spend some time with the Lord, thanking Him for the freedom He offers His children. Ask God to help you grab onto His powerful truth so you can chase away the doubts that Satan throws into your mind. Ask Him to help you let go of the thought patterns and bad habits that keep you from reflecting that you are a new creature in Christ. Ask Him to free you from beating yourself up in your struggle with sin. Tell God that you want to be a light in this dark world, and thank Him for the fact that victory is truly there for us through Jesus Christ our Lord!

You Can Win the Battle for Your Mind

Think About Your Own Battle

In chapter 3, Dan and Neil had a conversation about the struggle in Dan's mind over his feelings about who he was. As they read through the Scripture from Romans 7, Dan began to see himself in a new light.

He was asking the same question that so many young believers have: "If what the Bible says about who I am in Christ is true, then how come I still struggle with the same thoughts and feelings I did before I became a Christian?"

- Have you wrestled with this question yourself? Think about it again (or for the first time) before you go on.

  — What does the apostle Paul tell believers in regard to their minds?

  — In Romans 12:2, who do you think is doing the transforming?

Strongholds of Self-Defense

In our life before Christ, we learned many ways to cope or to defend ourselves that were not always healthy. These "defense mechanisms" are similar to what Paul calls "fortresses" or "strongholds." Strongholds are fleshly thought patterns that were programmed into our minds when we learned to live independently of God.

- What is the answer to our problem with strongholds? How can we "unlearn" them?

- Look again at Morgan's story on pages 65–66 of the text.
  — What can you learn from Morgan's experience?

  — How did Morgan allow God to renew her mind and free it from the old patterns?

  — Look at the nine thoughts that Morgan had as she battled the temptation to vomit. Which of these truths can you add to your arsenal so you'll be able to stand strong the next time you're facing temptation from an old flesh pattern or from the devil?

There is a war raging, but you are on the winning side, for you are more than a conqueror in Christ!

Satan's Schemes

Even though you're on the winning side, Satan is still interested in manipulating your mind in order to get his work done. He knows

Not a Friend

There's a difference between being friendly to others and being close friends with everyone. One you can do, or at least aspire to. The other is simply impossible.

We human beings aren't made to be intimate companions with the whole human race. That's an insight that mostly comes with maturity. Friendship is a precious thing to be guarded and valued, not carelessly dispensed nor cavalierly treated.

It's important to remember, too, that not everyone is a friend who claims to be one.

The waiter who gives us his name and insists on engaging us in conversation—he's not necessarily our friend.

The airplane seatmate who tells us the story of her life—she's not necessarily our friend.

The telemarketer who chats amiably before settling down to her spiel—she's almost certainly not our friend.

But these are superficial examples, minor annoyances.

More problematic is the colleague who invites our confidences, then spreads them behind our backs. More troubling is the acquaintance who claims to love us dearly but consistently forgets our birthday and can't keep our children straight and just doesn't have time to help when we have a problem. More disturbing is the associate who always needs to talk but never can manage to listen.

These people are not true friends of any flavor. Anyone who takes her friendships seriously would be wise to guard against these kinds of false friendships.

A false friend is not just a friend who hurts us. Most friends manage to hurt and betray each other from time to time—that's why forgiveness is essential to any lasting friendship.

A false friend is something different. She is one who, for whatever reason, just doesn't have our best interest at heart, but who tries to hide her chronic ill will behind loving words and friendly gestures. Or she is one whose own self-centeredness makes her incapable of the give-and-take of friendship. Her path may parallel yours. You may run in the same circles and have civil exchanges, but the qualities of a true, intimate friendship—trust, openness, honesty, mutual caring—are just not there.

Sometimes a false friend is easy to recognize. Other times you don't have a clue until you find you've been betrayed. But it helps to keep your eyes open, especially to the way your friend treats others. (If she talks behind another person's back, who's to say she won't talk behind yours?) You usually can trust your instincts. If you feel uneasy in her company, perhaps there's a reason. You can remind yourself that true friendship is something that must be earned, and you don't owe everyone the gift of your friendship.

That is an important thing to keep in mind, although many people misunderstand.

It is important to be kind and polite to whomever crosses our path. It's important to show love and compassion to people in need. But it is simply folly to accept everyone as a true friend.

We can learn from false friends—especially lessons in how *not* to treat people.

We can even feel for them, for false friends are often people in pain.

But we don't have to give them our trust.

We don't even have to give them much of our time.

We don't have to hold them close to our hearts.

It's one thing to be friendly.

But it's simply not necessary—nor is it wise—to be everyone's friend.

True friends are too precious for us to squander our trust and our time on those whose friendship is false.

Beautiful Music Together

What a delight to learn something new about an old friend!

Even more delightful is to discover something the two of us have had in common all along . . . and never knew till now.

That's how we felt on the afternoon when we found out we had both played the cello as girls.

"You're kidding! You, too?"

"I can't believe it."

Neither of us was first-chair material, and neither of us has held a bow in many a year. But we both dearly loved the process of making music on that wonderful, mellow instrument. And we both were thrilled to be involved in the creation, however imperfect, of something truly beautiful.

The more we thought about it, in fact, the more we realized that's exactly what we're doing as we live and share as friends.

We're collaborating on a lovely, joyful, unique work of art.

If our friendship were music, it would be a wonderful duet—a composition for four hands.

If it were a painting, it would be a collaborative canvas— a landscape colored with dual brushes.

If it were a tapestry, it would be woven with two dancing shuttles—the threads of our days and moments and our single and shared threads combining to create surprising and unforgettable patterns.

We don't want to go overboard with the metaphors here! But the point is that all friendship is a joint creation—a beautiful thing we create over time, together.

We craft it from the simplest materials: our words and our silences and our silliness and our sacrifice and our gifts and our gestures. And we take turns sounding the notes and wielding the brush and weaving the thread.

You give. I take. Then we switch places.

There are some times when you take the lead, other times when I do. Sometimes we plan where our collaboration is going; other times we improvise joyfully.

I invite you to come visit me, and we share a cup of tea.

You tell a funny story. I listen and laugh. Then I tell one.

I see you are hurting and try to help. You hear my need and send me an encouraging note.

You counsel my children. I hold you up in prayer.

That's the way it goes: One mellow note, then another answering. One stroke of color, then another beside it. A change of thread, a sweep of the shuttle.

Bit by bit, something lovely is created, and most of the time it doesn't even feel like work. Often it feels like fun. And almost always, even in the midst of trouble, there's a sense of elation.

It's a joy to create something beautiful. And it's a joy to be part of a miracle—because all intimate friendships, like all works of true art, have a bit of the miraculous about them.

Maybe it's because we know that this beautiful thing we created together is somehow more than we are.

Maybe our enthusiastic brush strokes have been touched up while we slept.

Maybe our dancing shuttles have been guided by a Master Weaver.

Maybe our mellow duet has been a trio all along—with the true Source of these heavenly harmonies!

We think so, anyway. Because we know this work of art that is our friendship is far more beautiful than anything the two of us second-chair friends could manage!

Something to ponder . . .

*To me, my most treasured friendships
can be compared to . . .*

20 Questions (to Ask a Friend)

These questions provide a fun forum for getting to know your new friends and getting to know your old friends better. Use them for party games, for conversation starters. For an old and treasured friend, see how many you can guess about her!

1. Where did your family live when you were six? When you were 12?
2. What was your favorite subject in school?
3. Have you ever played a musical instrument? What was it?
4. What is your favorite sport? Did you ever play it—or did you prefer to watch?
5. What was your least favorite food as a child?
6. Name your first boyfriend. How old were you when you met?
7. If you were beginning life again and could choose any career, what would you choose?
8. What is the most valuable thing you've learned in the past ten years?
9. What lost person or thing in your life do you miss the most?
10. What is the most encouraging word anyone can say to you?
11. Describe the most wonderful vacation you've ever taken. Why was it so great?
12. In what areas of your life do you feel most successful? Least successful?
13. What was the loneliest moment of your life? Why?
14. What single accomplishment in your life have you been proudest of?
15. What is your favorite season of the year and why?
16. Name an older person (not your parents) who influenced you as a younger person.
    What did you learn from that person?
17. If you had an unlimited budget to remodel just one room in your house, what would you do? In which room?
18. What was your favorite song when you were 16?
19. If you had to spend a year alone on a desert island and could take just three things with you, what would you take?
20. What's your idea of a truly perfect morning? What would you do?

"You must be a friend," said Corduroy.
"I've always wanted a friend."
"Me too!" said Lisa, and
gave him a big hug.

—DON FREEMAN,
Corduroy

2

"Remember When We Met?"

How Friendships Get Started

"A [woman] that hath friends must
show [herself] friendly."
—THE BOOK OF PROVERBS

Once Upon a Time

All stories have to begin somewhere. And so all friendships have their tales of "how we got together in the first place."

Sometimes the beginnings are murky, shrouded in childhood mists or simply faded in the distance. Some friends can't recall a time when they weren't together.

But often the stories of our beginnings are clear and vivid—memory milestones. And just as children cherish the stories of their birth as reminders of how valued they are in a family, we think friends ought to cherish the tales of their beginnings. These tales are fun to tell, and valuable because they remind us of why we're friends in the first place.

Not every friendship story begins with "once upon a time." Every beginning is different, as unique as the friendship, although most tales of beginning do follow a familiar path.

First there's a meeting: "Once upon a time there were two people." Usually it's face-to-face—an introduction, a chance encounter, or simply finding yourself in the same place at the same time. Friendships begin in grade-school classrooms, in workplace restrooms, in church nurseries, in soccer-field bleachers. It's possible to meet by telephone (we did) or by mail or even by reputation ("You really need to meet so-and-so; I just know you would love each other").

Once you've met, in order for an encounter to develop into a friendship, somebody has to reach out, to take the next step. It could be as simple as a question that sparks a conversation or a compliment that warms a heart:

> "Do you have any other children?"
> "Where did you grow up?"
> "I really admire your work on that sampler."

Or it could be an invitation:

> "Would you like to have lunch with me tomorrow?"
> "A group of us likes to go to this antique shop. Would you like to come?"
> "Want to grab a cup of coffee and talk?"

And then, if the friendship is going to work, the other person has to respond with some kind of a yes. Not perhaps to a specific question or invitation, but yes to the possibility of friendship.

Next comes one of the most fun parts in a beginning friendship. Remember that charming little song from *The King and I*, "Getting to Know You"? That's what you're doing in those days when you are exchanging stories and discovering each other.

It's almost like a courtship—a little dance. It's a series of offers and responses, of questions and answers, of give-and-take. With every interaction you are learning "beautiful and new" things about one another.

Then one day, at some point along the way, you realize that your "once upon a time" has launched itself into a full-fledged tale of friendship.

Now, some stories start right at the beginning, while others meander into the heart of the tale at a leisurely pace. And that's true of friendships, too.

Sometimes the "getting to know you" period is so abbreviated you almost don't know it's there. You have the sense that you were friends from the moment you met . . . or even before.

Other times, the courtship is prolonged—you remain for days or months or years as colleagues or casual acquaintances or people who once met or people who like each other but somehow can't manage to get together. And then one day, for some reason, you click. You start talking and you can't stop. Or you run into each other at your child's ball game and have such a fabulous time sitting together that you can't understand why you didn't get together before. Or you happen to share a crisis or a challenge that throws you together and draws you close.

It doesn't really matter how or when it happens. It's the variations in the story that make it so interesting and wonderful. It's the twists and turns that make the story worth telling.

But you know when you've reached the heart of the story! A spark has fired and it's lit a warm fire in your hearts, and you're beginning to enjoy and to trust and to love each other, and something tells you this is going to last awhile.

And then you can begin looking back together and telling each other, "Remember when it first began?"

A Friendship Story

"When my best friend, my life partner for 12 years, died suddenly and unexpectedly at age 54, I turned to the Internet for support. I dropped into the family forum on CompuServe and found a few others to communicate with. A few weeks later a cry of help from a 'new widow' appeared.

"We wrote back and forth sharing our stories—her husband had had a heart attack at his daughter's wedding—and our feelings. We sent each other pictures of ourselves and our spouses. We became the single most important support person for each other during the very difficult grieving process, and we are still in touch today. We wrote notes daily until recently and now write several times a week; the record serves as my journal. It's been almost two years.

"We have never met. I live in Oregon and she lives in Eastern Canada. Despite that, I know I have made a special friend for life, and we know as much about each other as our local friends do. I wouldn't be the same without her."

—Sally J. Mann,
Eugene, Oregon

You Never Know

Our own story started with friends of friends.

A woman Emilie knew in Riverside kept mentioning that *her* friend in Arizona knew someone Emilie would really like.

And a friend of Donna's in Phoenix kept talking about this great woman in California that a friend of hers had met.

"You've got so much in common."

"I know you would just love each other!"

"You really ought to call."

The problem was: we just weren't all that interested!

Each of us had too much going on in her life (we thought) to worry about making friends with a woman who lived in a completely different state and had a completely different life.

But Emilie's friend kept talking to Donna's friend. And those friends kept urging us to get together. And finally one of us made the phone call.

It was fine. We enjoyed the conversation. And that was that. Remember, we really didn't have time to worry about making friends with a woman who lived in a completely different state and had a completely different life.

Except one phone call led to another. And we discovered we really did have a lot in common. And after a fair number of long-distance phone calls we even began to wonder if we should work together. At that time Emilie's home-management business was really beginning to take off and she was considering selling franchises. Perhaps Donna should take over a franchise.

So Donna flew to Riverside to meet Emilie and sit in on a seminar. And we talked a lot. We found out we really liked each other, although we still didn't know if the franchise idea would work.

Well, the upshot was that the franchise idea *didn't* work, but the friendship did. Today the two of us enjoy separate (though similar) careers, but our lives are anything but separate. We've decided we just can't afford not to be friends. And even though we live in completely different states, we have managed to keep a lively friendship going for more than 18 years.

When did we know it was going to happen?

As we remember, it was really two different moments.

For Emilie, it happened on Donna's first visit, when Donna sat down and spelled out, "This is what I do: A, B, C." Emilie thought, *I like this person. She's really organized. And I can't believe she took the trouble to come all the way out here and talk to me.*

For Donna, it came a little later, while we were still negotiating about the possibility of a franchise. Donna asked a very pointed question: "What if I go with you now but later on I decide to branch out and hold seminars on my own?" Emilie's answer was that that would be fine—there's plenty of room out there for both of us. And Donna remembers thinking, *I like this person. I can't believe she's so generous and gracious.*

By that time, we were well on the way to becoming close friends.

And what did we learn from the unusual start of our story?

Simply that it's a good idea to keep your eyes and heart open . . . because you never know where your next close friend is coming from!

Beginning Stories

*I*n many ways," writes Sharon J. Wohlmuth in the introduction to her book *Best Friends*, "[friendship] is all the more precious because something so powerful can spring from origins as elusive as a chance meeting or a shared interest." Here are some stories our friends have told us of how they met. How did your most treasured friendships start?

- ☙ Emilie met her friend Barbara D. Lorenzo while delivering product from a home business. Something about Barbara's house caught Emilie's eye, and she thought, *I could like a person who lives in that house.*

- ☙ Donna met her friend Sandy when they both agreed to be part of a friendship covenant group. They met at the very first group meeting, and Sandy's still a treasured friend.

- ☙ Marilyn and Linda were introduced by Linda's real-estate agent right after Linda moved to town. They bonded at first because they were Midwesterners transplanted into a Southwestern town, then discovered mutual interests in cooking, antiques, and the arts. But it was nine years of sharing a daily walk (and drinking coffee) that really cemented their friendship.

- ☙ Anne met Debra working after hours at work. Debra had just been hired and was putting her new office together. Anne was plugging away at her desk when Debra came foraging for a hammer. The best Anne could do was a stapler . . . but the friendship has held together fine!

ℒ♥ Maxine was surprised to become friends at work with a woman she had known from a distance in high school—a woman she had always thought of as an unapproachable "popular person." All it really took was a chance to talk together outside of their previous roles. Then they discovered they shared a spiritual commitment and an interest in writing. They've been friends ever since.

Something to ponder . . .

If I were to write a story of how a special friendship began, this is how it would go . . .

A Friendship Story

"When I was in fifth grade, I met my best friend Victoria. She and I were both recently fatherless, shy, and nonremarkable in many ways. As the years passed, we grew in the most beautiful friendship and sisterhood. We shared everything together: secrets, crushes on boys, our insecurities, and all manner of secrets that young women share. . . . Truly God used us to help each other grow, not only in our youth, but in spiritual matters as well. As the years passed, our friendship thrived through our teen years, and beyond to our twenties. We both wound up living in Vancouver, Washington, at the same time with our spouses and families. I saw her on a regular basis.

"When we were 28 (17 years after we met), Victoria died suddenly from a pulmonary embolism on Easter morning. For several years, I wondered how I could survive without her friendship, but her mark is as strong on my soul now as it was in our childhood. I still hear her in my memories and in my heart, loving, understanding, and encouraging me to be that person that God made and intended me to be. She will never be on this earth again, but this makes my home-coming to heaven all the sweeter, as I not only will see my Lord, but my dearest friend as well."

—Carol Ann Hickman,
Junction City, Oregon

Choosing or Chosen?

Do you choose your friendships—or do your friendships choose you?

It's probably a little bit of both—or it should be.

Sometimes it does feel like you were destined to be together, that you are instant friends with someone without having anything to say in the matter. It's almost as if God chose the two of you to be together and gave you your friendship as a gift. But you still chose to say yes to the friendship, to invest your time and energy toward nurturing it.

Sometimes, on the other hand, you feel like one of you is the chooser and the other is the chosen. In fact, most friendships begin, we believe, when one person chooses to pursue the other as a friend. In our friendship it was Donna who took the initiating role. But both of us have played chooser and chosen roles in friendships. At times we have switched roles within our own relationship.

There's always an element of choice in making and keeping friends. And just as your mother probably told you, it's vitally important to choose the right friends.

Now, some people really resist this idea. To them, choosing friends sounds somehow elitist, as if you were gazing down your nose from Mount Olympus and selecting those people who are good enough to associate with or picking the winner at a beauty contest or squeezing all the cantaloupes in the market to find the ripest one.

But that's not really what choosing friends mean. It's not a matter of judging people, then picking some and rejecting the others. We all have met plenty of perfectly splendid persons who for one reason or another didn't become our close friends.

The way we see it, choosing friends is simply part of being responsible human beings. It's part of facing the reality that our time and our energy—even our stay on this earth—is finite, and that investing it wisely means learning to focus. Trying to spread ourselves among too many people almost inevitably means developing deep, intimate relationships with none. So it makes sense to choose to spend time with relationships that truly nourish the souls of both of you.

Choosing friends, then, is also a part of knowing ourselves, realizing that certain associations strengthen us, teach us, and fill our needs, while others push our buttons or feed our weaknesses. It's part of caring for ourselves, realizing that we really do need the support of those who share our values and "fill our cups."

All this means that it's a good idea to have a picture of what is important to you in a friend. It helps to know what you can live with and what you can't, what's really important to you and what you can let slide.

It's not elitist to face the fact that lazy people tend to drive you crazy, or that loud people make you cringe, or that you just can't trust someone who can't remember your birthday. (Someone else may actually prefer a friend who is less driven, more enthusiastic, who doesn't follow the rules.)

It's not elitist to realize that a chronic complainer tends to bring out the whine in you, too. (Someone else might easily be able to resist the whine while enjoying the generosity and genuine thoughtfulness that go along with that particular complainer.)

It's certainly not elitist to realize that hanging out with compulsive shoppers tends to wreak havoc with your budget resolves! Sometimes you simply have to recognize your limits.

Remember, when you choose your friends, you're not choosing whom you will talk to, whom you will associate with, whom you will reach out to or help or show kindness to.

You're deciding whom you will trust with your heart and your soul.

You're deciding who will work with you as you try to accomplish what you were put on earth to do.

You're deciding who can handle and accept and love the you beneath the surface.

And it's a simple fact that not everyone qualifies for that very specialized position, just as you may not be qualified to fill it in some people's lives.

But lest this sound too heavy, remember that you're almost never required to make these choices all at once. Usually you make a series of small choices that lead you down the path toward friendship. And usually there are plenty of opportunities along the way to back out if you feel the friendship simply isn't working.

Here's how it typically goes:

First, you choose, consciously or unconsciously, to open your mind to the possibility of a friendship.

Then you choose to take the next step. You smile. You say hello. You respond. And then you make the phone call or issue the invitation, and the other person reciprocates.

With each step you are choosing to move forward with the friendship or to pull away.

And here's the really good news.

You have the opportunity all your life to continue to choose loving, supportive, trustworthy friends. You even have the opportunity to change your mind, to decide that the quality you just can't live with is overshadowed by an even more sterling quality you just can't live without.

And the best part of all is realizing your friend feels the same about you.

After all, she chose you as a friend.

Finding Friends

There are times in our lives when choosing friends seems less of an issue than finding them in the first place.

These are usually the transition times. Maybe you've moved to a new house or a new town or even across the country. Or maybe you've been widowed or divorced or your children have grown and you've changed jobs. Whenever you pass a milestone or go through a change, you might find that you have less in common with your old friends, or that they're just too far away to come over on the spur of the moment to share a cup of tea and a good cry.

Those can be lonely times—those days when you're feeling short of friends. You really feel the lack of someone to shop with, someone to chat over the fence with, someone to call for a lunch date. You feel a little awkward starting over again with people who don't know you from Eve.

But here's the good news: These lonely times can also be growing times. They're times of opportunity and promise, when new acquaintances can add freshness to your life. You can reinvent yourself as you develop new relationships. You can look back over your past and perhaps correct old mistakes. You can practice faith and patience, because you really can't hurry the natural process of getting to know others.

And you can remember (for this is true) that the lonely times usually don't last.

In the meantime, there are some things you can do to make it all a little easier.

First of all, make use of your lifelines. These are the ties you still maintain: your friends from your previous job, your long-time friends who live far away, your family, your dog. This is not the time in your life to worry about the phone bill.

This is not the time to hole up and hide. Write letters. Keep up contact with the people who love you, even if they don't fill your need for close-up friends. Solicit their prayers. Ask them to visit. If at all possible, arrange to make your own visits.

Second (this is the obvious one) take steps to put yourself in friendship's way. Consider joining organizations, volunteering for jobs, pursuing interests you might not have pursued before. It's hard to make new friends while you're sitting at home.

Third, try to reach out. If you meet someone you like, make a friendly overture. Smile or say hello. Ask her to lunch. Invite her to go somewhere with you. When someone else speaks to you, respond. Say yes when you can. Give yourself a chance to get to know the other person.

It helps to open your mind to friendship possibilities you might not have considered. A friend doesn't have to be someone just like you. In fact, some of our most fulfilling, enduring friendships have been with someone who is older . . . or younger . . . or from a different walk in life.

A stay-at-home mom can be friends with a mother who works outside the home. A Ph.D. really can resonate with a high-school graduate if you have other things in common. An older widow who lives alone can develop a fulfilling friendship with the young couple across the street.

So don't limit yourself as you look for friends. Say hello to someone who appeals to you, even if she's not what you've always considered "friend material." You never know who might turn out to be your next bosom buddy.

And here's something we've found to be very helpful in those transitional, low-friend times. When you find yourself short on intimate nearby friends, try to make a point of being thankful for what you do have.

For instance, you can say thank you for any companionship, even if it doesn't blossom into full-fledged friendship.

Not all your encounters will click, but it's still nice to have someone to run with or drink coffee with or talk to in class. Besides, you never know what future friendships will spring from present acquaintances.

You can also say thank you for the free time that a shortage of friends may bring. This can be a time to explore your own heart, to read and learn something new, to enjoy those interests that your former friends might not have shared. Now is a time to reflect on the kind of friend you've been in the past and resolve to be a better friend in the future. Chances are, your life will soon be filled once again with the privileges and obligations of friendship. Now is a time to enjoy the quiet.

You can even say thank you, as well, for the empty space that has opened up in your life. It may not feel like a blessing, but it very well might be. Perhaps that space is there for a purpose—it's waiting to be filled by a future friend of the heart. So instead of rushing to fill the friendship void in your life, you might try leaving it open for a little while. Think of it as leaving room for future friendships God has in mind for you.

Then wait. Pray. Hold onto your lifelines and put yourself in friendship's way, but don't push too hard. Practice trusting that you'll be granted the friendship you need when you need it.

Believe it.

You will.

Where to Meet Friends

❧ on a bench at the playground

❧ at an elderhostel

❧ in a choir

❧ at the library

❧ at church

❧ at a museum

❧ at a committee meeting

❧ in the break room at work

❧ at a softball game

❧ at a Bible study or study group

❧ in the produce department of the grocery store

❧ on the beach

❧ at a prayer group

❧ at a pottery studio

❧ at another friend's house

What to Do with a New Friend

❧ exercise

❧ go to a movie

❧ shop

❧ clean house together

❧ meet for coffee or tea

❧ take a walk in the park

❧ visit a day spa

❧ pray

❧ read and discuss a book

❧ browse for books or antiques

❧ share a picnic

❧ take the kids on an outing

A Friendship Story

"Having heart-to-heart friendships has always been very important to me. I have been truly blessed as each friendship has grown over time, through various trials. So when we had to move away from our lifelong hometown, it was difficult to think of leaving my friends and having the energy to cultivate new ones.

"On our first house hunting visit to the new area, we attended church on Sunday. There I met a warm and friendly woman named Fran. . . . She gave me names and information, including her name and phone number. Somehow when she said to call her if I needed anything, I sensed she really meant it.

"In the months before we actually moved, I contacted her a couple more times, we met at lunch, and we both felt a special bond of friendship already growing. She showed up at our house the day we moved in and was a tremendous practical support to me in the first weeks as I needed help in a totally new environment. Although we only lived there eight months, our husbands also became friends. I was amazed at how the Lord blessed us with such a 'fast' friendship.

"I am glad I had the courage to reach out in my time of need, and I thank God for sending a warm hand to take hold of mine. It takes two!"

—Cathie McCormick,
Venetia, Pennsylvania

"I Have All the Friends I Need"

In a sense, you can't ever have too many friends.

But both of us have had times in our lives when our hearts felt closed to the possibility of new involvements.

Sometimes we've felt like we didn't have enough time or energy for anyone outside our families and our work and our small circle of old friends.

Other times we were grieving the deeply felt loss of a good friend, and something in us rebelled at the idea of filling up her place.

Have you ever felt that way—as if your heart was just too full for one more good friend?

Well, there's wisdom, of course, in knowing your limits.

But there's also wisdom in keeping a corner of your heart open to the new.

Maybe we believe this because our own friendship started in one of those too-full times. What a shame it would have been to miss this relationship just because our lives were so full!

But how do you keep your heart open when it wants to be closed?

We've found that it helps to keep an open-ended view of life—remembering that every life is an unfinished painting until the final brush strokes are taken. You still don't know all the major elements that will form the composition of your life.

You're still in progress, and there will be changes. And the relationships that call to you today may well be the ones that carry you through the next phase of development.

An unfinished painting is far more evocative and haunting than a finished one. Something in that empty space—the areas that are sketched but not colored, or blocked in but not finished—speaks of possibilities and promise.

When you look at your life that way—as still in progress, not as sewn-up and unchangeable—you'll find your heart stays more open to new friendships.

And when you do that . . . you'll find that new possibilities are always right around the corner.

Connecting . . . 18 Great Ideas for Meeting New Friends and Getting to Know Them Better

Whether you're a newcomer or an old hand, these ideas can help you connect with potential friends.

1. *Carry a card.* Keep a small supply of business cards or personal calling cards in your purse. That way, if you meet a new friend, it's easy to say, "Call me." Don't forget to jot down the new friend's name and number on another card for you to keep.

2. *Drop a line.* Keep a little basket of note cards or post-cards, a pen, and some stamps in a convenient spot. If you meet someone you would like to know better, drop her a note and tell her so. If you have a computer, send off a quick e-mail.

3. *Issue an invitation.* The only way to get past the level of small talk is to schedule some time together. Invite a new acquaintance to lunch, to tea, or just to share a coffee break. Or invite her along on a shopping trip or an afternoon workout.

4. *Give a compliment.* When you see something you like, develop the habit of saying so. Nothing warms the heart of a potential friend like feeling appreciated.

5. *Take notes.* If you're reaching the age where you tend to forget details, actually write down important things you learn about a new acquaintance: her husband's name, her birthday, her children's ages, where she lived before.

6. *Offer a welcome.* It's hard to move into a new community or area. If someone new moves into your neighborhood, community, or church, take a minute for an

old-fashioned gesture of welcome. A basket full of maps, coupons, and treats speaks a wonderful welcome, but even a store-bought pie or a plate of bakery cookies can break the ice and jump-start friendship.

7. *Open your mind.* Your next best friend just might be someone you don't expect—perhaps someone older, younger, or simply different.

8. *If you click, connect.* Sometimes you'll find yourself striking up a conversation with a stranger in the beauty shop, in the grocery store line, or at the playground. Don't let that potential friend walk away! Ask her to go for a cup of coffee, or exchange phone numbers or e-mail addresses.

9. *Leave room in your life for future friends.* Try scheduling some things to do alone on a regular basis—a walk in the neighborhood, an hour in the garden, a moment for tea—with the idea that you might share that time later with a new friend.

10. *Introduce friends to friends.* Your circle of friends is bound to enlarge, and you may meet some special new people in the process. In fact, why not throw a party and ask each guest to bring a friend from a different walk of life?

11. *Learn something new.* Take a class, buy a how-to book, join a study group, contact an expert who knows something you want to know. The more you ask questions and participate in your new interest, the more potential friends you're apt to meet.

12. *Nourish spiritual connections.* Attend worship, or join a study or prayer group. If you meet someone who seems to share your interest in spiritual matters, ask if she would consider sharing with you on a regular basis.

13. *Join a group, or start one.* One of the best ways to meet friends is to join a group of people you have something in common with: a "Mommy and Me" group, a quilter's guild, a rock collector's meeting. How do you find a group? Look in the newspaper, ask at the public library, inquire at shops (a needlework shop might host a needlework group), or surf the net (a national organization might list a local meeting). If you can't find a group, post a message on a bulletin board to find someone who might be interested in starting one with you.

14. *Build on common ground.* If you meet someone whose circumstances or interests are similar to yours, suggest pooling resources. Perhaps you could clean house together (half the time at each house), share yard work, walk your dogs together, or gather all the kids into one yard for games and conversation. You'll take care of necessary tasks while building a relationship.

15. *Ask for help with a project.* It's not only a good way to get the job done; it's also a nice way to get to know someone better.

16. *Offer someone a ride* to a meeting or other gathering. The gesture is usually appreciated, and the commute is a nice time to get to know each other better.

17. *Make friends on the job.* Working together is a great way to make new friends, and this is true whether the job is a volunteer committee spot or a full-time career. If you find yourself low on friends and you have the time, consider getting a job of some kind. Then if you "click" with a coworker, ask her to share a cup of coffee or an off-duty dinner.

18. *Keep a yes in your heart.* You never know whether the next person you meet will turn out to be a dear chosen sister.

*"I'll talk all day if you'll
only set me going. Beth says
I never know when to stop."*

—LOUISA MAY ALCOTT,
Little Women

3

"I Always Laugh When I'm with You"

On Being Together

"But it was you . . . my companion. . . .
We took sweet counsel together."

—The Book of Psalms

Playing Together

"Can you come out and play?"

Remember when those were the words you wanted most to hear?

When we were little, after all, the central purpose of having friends was having someone to play with.

Our play was really our work, of course. It was the way we learned. But oh, how we loved to do it together: riding bikes, jumping rope, dressing our dolls, playing make-believe.

Remember what it was like to play with your friends?

You still need that feeling in your life.

You need fun in your friendships, for that quality of play is what lifts you and renews you and refreshes you. You need friends to go to movies with (especially the ones your husband or male friend just won't go to), to shop garage sales with, to share cookouts with your family, to talk with on the phone, or just to sit with and enjoy a beautiful afternoon and a cup of tea and some laughter.

Maybe not every friend is a fun friend. Some friendships seem to exist just to share adversity. And certainly a sturdy friendship will have far more to it than shared amusement. But the deepest friendships, as far as we've been able to tell, are almost always fertilized by fun. Almost always, friends of the heart are friends who play together.

What you do for fun, of course, will depend on who you are together, what interests you share. It will depend on what you need, what diversions bring you relaxation and joy . . . certainly on what the two of you have in common.

Some friends play games. Donna's sweet mother-in-law had a group of friends—they called themselves "the girls"—who met in kindergarten and grew up together and then met regularly for bridge games until Mom moved to Arizona at age 76. Those friends and games were a support group, a source of therapy as well as fun for all those years.

Other friends love to share physical activity: tennis or racquetball or mall-walking or bungee jumping. (Whether this is fun or not will depend on your point of view, but even shared misery can be a great friendship-builder!) The two of us have always loved to share walks when we're together—talking nonstop or just enjoying each other's companionship as we walk the canal path beneath the orange blossoms in Riverside or hike up into Phoenix's red desert mountains.

Some friends have fun sharing hobbies: decorating, needlework, pottery, even woodworking. (We like to cook and read magazines and go to movies and go antiquing.) Some friends make music together . . . or create new recipes together . . . or play games with the children or grandchildren . . . or garden side by side.

Some friends share adventures and collect stories for future telling, like the time Emilie and her friend Yoli decided to take Yoli's husband's kayak out on the bay in Newport Beach. They were not the best and most experienced of rowers, and they spent most of that outing going backwards. But when they were through, they pulled the kayak up on the shore and lay down and just laughed and laughed.

And laughter is surely a healing, restorative part of the fun that comes with friendship. Our best friends, we find, are the ones we can laugh with. It's the laughter that lubricates our irritations, that releases our tensions, that feeds our joy. Whether it comes from gentle teasing (Emilie's husband, Bob, and Donna love to rib each other!) or funny anecdotes or cartoons clipped from the paper or just silliness and giggles . . . it's the laughter that helps keep things warm and joyful, even in the midst of pain.

Celebration, too, is part of the fun. Celebrating milestones. Celebrating accomplishments. Celebrating the fact that it's a beautiful day and you are friends. Whether you are a party person or you prefer quieter ceremonies of rejoicing, you feed your friendships with fun whenever you stage a celebration. That's why we recommend, whenever possible, that you celebrate extravagantly and enthusiastically. Bring out the balloons and the confetti. Deliver solemn speeches and lots of hugs. Wear silly hats.

Silliness, as a matter of fact, adds a special quality to the fun in any friendship. That's because it takes a lot of trust to let down your guard and be truly silly, even with someone you love. You're letting yourself be a child again, and trusting your child-self to another person. When you feel free to act absolutely silly with a friend, you understand most fully the freedom a friendship can grant.

Have you ever grabbed a friend and gone to the park to swing?

Or shared impersonations of people you both know?

Or sat down on the floor with a bunch of coloring books and colored to your heart's content?

Or bought yourself a balloon to carry through the mall?

Count yourself blessed if you have a friend who doesn't mind—or, even better, wants to do it with you.

For that matter, you should count yourself blessed for all the fun you have with any of your friends.

For fun isn't frivolous, any more than play is frivolous for a child.

Fun is an important reward of friendship.

It's part of the gift you give each other—the gift of abundant joy.

Friends Share . . .

- ❧ recipes
- ❧ beauty tips
- ❧ exercise
- ❧ secrets
- ❧ back rubs
- ❧ shopping trips
- ❧ desserts
- ❧ long walks
- ❧ household hints
- ❧ ideas
- ❧ child care

- ❧ chores
- ❧ phone calls
- ❧ clothes (sometimes)
- ❧ cards and letters
- ❧ each other's friends
- ❧ minutes, days, and hours
- ❧ problems to be solved
- ❧ heartaches
- ❧ joys
- ❧ themselves

Something to ponder . . .

*This is something I love to share
with my friend . . .*

A Friendship Story

"Our family recently relocated to Pennsylvania from Arizona, and leaving my close friends was particularly difficult and painful. After our move, five of my dear girlfriends found a unique way to keep in touch and make me feel loved and missed. My husband had called these friends and asked them to plan a fortieth birthday/girlfriend bash for me because his gift to me was a trip to California and Arizona to celebrate with friends and family. . . .

"I was greeted at the airport by these normally attractive, well-dressed girlfriends in "*Old* Spice Girl" outfits. Their appearance was beyond description. Each outfit was complete with matching T-shirts with my picture, as a screaming two-year-old, on the front and the caption, 'Sherilyn is 40 but not a good sporty!' They had chosen personal "spice" names for each of us, neatly printed across our backs. My name was Paprika, but they referred to me as 'Reeka' and pronounced it only in a shrill scream.

"They whisked me away to a restroom in the airport and provided an outfit for me to change into. Soon I was adorned in skin-tight gold lamé bell-bottoms, four-inch white satin platform shoes with black tights, and a birthday T-shirt of my own. The outfit was complete with a sweet little tiara for my crown. They then paraded me all over town (movie, dinner, shopping mall) hootin' and hollerin' my spice name, my age, and many other birthday comments. We put big smiles on many faces!

"The remainder of the celebration included a two-night stay at a beautiful north Phoenix resort, a birthday cake, a manicure and pedicure, and hours of girl talk. It ended with another surprise party with many more friends, another costume (complete with a wig), a singing telegram by an old roommate, a skit, gifts, Mexican food (my favorite!) and more girl talk. It was a celebration like no other!

"Many of you may be thinking, 'If those are *friends*, I'd rather have enemies,' but you see, that's the glory of this tale; my friends knew that I would love such a celebration! I love people and I enjoy being crazy and having fun. That celebration was tailor-made for *me*; it was a labor of love. That is precisely what I cherish in these particular friendships."

—Sherilyn Jameson,
State College, Pennsylvania

Sharing the Load

Paintbrush in hand, Donna stood out in her yard next to her newly built, freshly stuccoed, unpainted fence and wondered if she would ever get it done in time.

Donna's husband, David, had built that fence himself over the past few weeks. Actually, it was more a wall than a fence, constructed of heavy concrete, and David had nearly crippled himself hauling and lifting the heavy blocks. Then the stucco man had come, and all that was left was to paint the fence. Donna really wanted to finish in time for David's birthday that night.

That's when the phone rang. It was Donna's friend Sue.

"Whatcha doing?"

Donna told her. And ten minutes later Sue had arrived with paintbrush in hand, ready to work.

The fence was beautifully painted long before party time. David was thrilled with the finished fence. And Donna was warmed and encouraged by this reminder of what a privilege it is to share the workload of life with a generous, dedicated friend.

Sharing the load. That's just as vital a part of friendship as sharing the fun. And though it may be true that woman's work is never done, it's also true that we women have always been good at sweetening our tasks by helping each other when we can.

Working together, in fact, has always been an integral part of women's friendships.

Think of primitive women grinding corn side by side.

Think of pioneer women gathering for a quilting bee.

Think of your grandmother sitting on the porch with her friends and shelling peas or swapping stories over the back fence while the laundry flaps in the breeze.

And think of you and your friends doing whatever it is you do . . . together.

Maybe you're a quilter, too, and you love to gather at one friend's house to do your stitching.

Maybe you like to share mundane household chores—cleaning, cooking, laundry—with a friend. (We recommend it.)

Maybe you search for business projects or club work you can do as a team, or you turn your committee sessions into fun, but fruitful, social sessions.

If you're not in the habit of looking for ways to enjoy the company of friends while you work . . . well, then, that's something to explore. For there's something about working side by side that builds friendships like nothing else can. Working together not only lightens the burden; it also builds a shared history, and it helps you get to know each other better. In fact, there's no better way to learn a person's true character than to see her on the job.

When we were young wives and stay-at-home moms, we both learned the value of sharing housecleaning work with a friend. This, of course, was before we met, so we did this with other friends. We would get together at one house, clean house like mad, move over to another house and clean, then go get coffee together. Donna even made a pact with a special friend to clean together on Wednesdays while they prayed and fasted for their children. She and her friend maintained the pact for nearly three years. Their reward was a deeper sense of closeness to their children and to each other. As a bonus, the housework flew by twice as fast.

Of course, housecleaning is not the only kind of work that lends itself to cooperative arrangements. Almost any kind of chore—from painting the fence to stuffing envelopes to putting in a new drain—can be accomplished together. (We've never done plumbing together, but who's to say it can't be done?) And creative endeavors such as decorating a house or designing a publicity plan for the new museum show will almost always profit from the synergy of compatible minds.

And it's always possible, of course, for two friends to share a professional endeavor. We know a freelance writer who goes out of her way to procure assignments she can do with her best friend. The two of them live thousands of miles away from each other—in Minnesota and Texas—but they use the vehicle of shared work to give themselves more time together, sometimes with a tax write-off for phone calls!

As we see it, there are three basic ways that women can nurture friendships while working together, and we recommend seizing every opportunity.

First, you can get together to take care of tasks that are dull, repetitive, or just big and daunting. This can be anything from scrubbing floors to repainting walls to addressing Christmas cards to canning fruit. Teaming up to tackle your chores or projects together will almost always make the work fly by.

Second, you can use your creativity in searching out fun or challenging tasks for the two of you to do. Consider teaming up to direct a play, teach Sunday School, prepare a meal for the homeless, or take a college class. Whatever skills and concerns you share can become an opportunity for the two of you to grow closer and learn more about each other.

A third—and vital—way that friends can work together is to do what Donna's friend did: You can step into the breach and help when one person's workload turns into overload. Friends help friends, whether it's keeping the kids so she can make a work deadline, helping cook and clean when unexpected guests arrive, or answering the phone during an especially busy and stressful day.

Emilie still remembers the overwhelming gratitude she felt when she was in ill health and facing a huge holiday seminar . . . and Donna and David flew out at their own expense to help. For three days they carried boxes, stacked books, supervised volunteers, and ran interference for Emilie while she tried to keep her energy up. Donna's unquestioning willingness to step in and share the work was just about the best Christmas gift Emilie received that year.

However you decide to work together, with your friends, we believe you'll reap many of the same wonderful benefits we've discovered.

One, you get to enjoy one another's company—a great plus in itself.

Second, you'll probably feel less alone and less burdened. Just knowing that you have someone supporting you makes any workload a bit easier to bear.

Third, you get to know each other better than you ever could if all your interactions were merely social. You'll learn how your friend acts under pressure, how she approaches problems. And even if time pressures or difference in work styles lead to petty annoyances, you'll have the opportunity to work through these difficulties to a deeper level of understanding and trust. Working together gives you a chance to practice tolerance, patience, and forgiveness.

You're building your friendship . . . while you're getting things done.

Can you think of a more joyful or efficient way to work?

A Friendship Story

"Rose told me that she was pregnant. Less than two weeks later, I found out I was pregnant, too. It was so wonderful sharing such a blessed occasion with a good friend. When Rose would come over and need food *now* and then be picky about what I had to offer, I understood. We went through morning sickness together. We complained to each other when no one else wanted to hear it. (Yes, misery does love company!)

"Rose was due December 24; I was due January 7. We planned to watch each other's older kids(s) while we delivered the new one. . . . But God had a different plan.

"I got the flu and due to dehydration went into labor December 27. (Rose was still heavy with child.) . . . The first time they let me nurse Adam alone in my room . . . the nurse brought him to me and then returned almost immediately. She said, 'There's a woman walking through her labor out here and she wants to know if she can come in. She says her name is Rose.' . . .

"How sublime! . . . I had my precious gift from God at my breast and at the same time had the honor of experiencing labor with one of my best friends (she is also a gift from God). Several hours later I walked down to the labor and delivery area and . . . they let me go in. Jack was still 'wet behind the ears,' literally! They were weighing him and he was red and screaming. The bond I feel with both these little boys is amazing."

—Tammy Aragaki,
Phoenix, Arizona

Kindred in Spirit

We've been there so many times before
—the two of us together somewhere, in
Emilie's comfy garden room or Donna's
welcoming den, or in a restaurant or an airport or a shopping
mall, our heads together, our hearts joined, sharing a prayer
or a word of hope before we continue with our day.

For as long as we've been friends, you see, we've been aware
that the friendship we share is really a three-way relationship
consisting of Emilie, Donna, and the God we both love.

That is not to say you can't be friends without sharing a
faith. It happens all the time. People without any kind of
spiritual orientation manage to nurture powerful bonds of
caring. People with different religious beliefs manage to tran-
scend their differences and enjoy fruitful friendships. We've
seen it. We've done it, for we, too, have friends whom we
cherish but who do not share our faith.

And yet . . .

And yet we've found that the spiritual commonality that
undergirds our particular friendship does give it a kind of
strength and sweetness we don't experience in those other
friendships. The bond of our shared spiritual commitment
connects us at a much deeper, more powerful level than the
simple bonds of human attraction and affection.

We love the picture painted in the Book of Ecclesiastes:
"A threefold cord is not quickly broken" (4:12). To us, that is
a picture of the two of us entwined in a friendship that
includes God as a third member. It's like silken cords girded
with steel. We trust it. We cherish it.

Not that we always agree with each other regarding every
belief, every interpretation. We don't. But we do share an
orientation of belief and a devotion that is a fundamental part
of who we are. We are both Christians. Our Christian faith is

vital to both of us. And we find that our faith is a common thread that holds us together when things are difficult, that gives us strength in our togetherness, that makes this friendship more than an association of two people who do similar work and enjoy similar activities.

From the very first, there has been a sense of sacredness in what we share together—not just the prayers and the Bible study and the spiritual talk, but everything we do.

And we certainly don't spend all our time together with hands folded and heads bowed!

But that's exactly beside the point . . . which is that our relationship with the One who made us and saves us and sustains us is woven into all aspects of our relationship with each other. It is a part of us—a deep, harmonious chord that grounds the dancing music of our time together.

Yes, we do pray together and for each other. We rest secure in the knowledge that we are in each other's prayers.

Yes, we do talk about what we believe and what we have experienced as people of faith. We share the thoughts we've gleaned from reading Scripture and the insights we believe the Holy Spirit has given us.

Yes, we love to worship together when it is possible, to share the experience of praising our God.

But we also laugh together—sometimes until our stomachs hurt—over something we've heard or something we've remembered. And that laughter, too, is part of our shared faith. To us it is holy laughter.

We support each other, and that sense of support is buoyed by knowing we are both loved of God. We try to care for each other both emotionally and physically, even as we trust God to take care of us both. And to us that mutual care is a holy thing as well.

We go shopping together and visit with other friends, and even as we compare prices and serve tea, the commonality of our spirits informs our choices and our attitudes.

Quite simply, the way we *are* is born out of where we put our trust, and where we put our trust is the essence of our life together as friends.

In our experience, at least, kindred spirits draw even closer when they share a kindred faith.

A Circle of Love

When you marry, you marry more than a person. You also marry into a family and into a set of friends and acquaintances. Your circle of love intersects with his circle of love— and his people, in a sense, will become your people.

We believe that's true of friendships as well.

Although it's possible to maintain a friendship that is more or less separate from other connections, we don't believe it's usual or even desirable. It's certainly not easy. For no woman, to paraphrase John Donne, is an island. Every one of us exists in a network of connections: mother, father, sisters, brothers, spouse, and friends. And it's almost impossible to nurture a deep connection to another person without being connected to her network as well.

Most of the time, this is a joy.

Sometimes it's a bit of a struggle, for loving a friend doesn't guarantee you'll automatically enjoy spending time with her family or other friends.

But the kind of deep, enduring friendships we've come to appreciate the most are the ones in which we can open our arms to embrace each other's children, grandchildren, husbands, significant others, and friends.

One thing we've really appreciated about our friendship is that our men are involved in it as well. From the beginning, we've liked the fact that Bob and David approve of our friendship—they like us to be together. Now we enjoy being "couple friends," and the time we spend together as a foursome is usually fun and fulfilling. We also like the fact that our husbands enjoy each other's company. That frees us to spend more time doing "girl things" together.

We also love feeling like second parents to each other's children. Emilie's children and grandchildren are folded into

Donna's heart. Donna's daughter is like Emilie's own child. And this is a wonderful gift, especially in those times when we cannot seem to talk to our own children. We cherish having someone who loves them almost as much as we do, who will care for them and guide them and speak the truth to them in love when we cannot speak it or they cannot hear it from our own lips. And we didn't really do it on purpose, but now we can see that our children have learned about friendship by watching us. Emilie's daughter Jenny told Donna recently, "I love watching you and my mom be friends!"

As for the friends of our friends . . . we have had such fun meeting and spending time with the people in each other's lives. After all, if they have something in common with our friend, they're likely to have something in common with us as well!

That doesn't mean that we have all become the closest of friends. Emilie has some dear friends that Donna just hasn't bonded with, and vice versa. We know other women friends whose husbands don't get along that well or whose children resist friendly overtures or whose close friends just can't see what they see in other friends.

We don't think that has to be a problem, necessarily. Friends don't have to share everything in common . . . even the people they love.

But even when we can't share affection, we can honor our friends' friends and family.

Usually it's enough to respect their commitments and not make our friends feel torn between us and the other people they love. Usually it's enough to be cordial and gracious when we meet the others in our friends' lives and to show them caring and compassion for friendship's sake.

Even in those rare cases when we feel another friend or a family member poses a danger, we are wise to choose our words carefully, weighing our honest concerns with our understanding.

But the good news is that, most of the time, this is simply not a problem.

Most of the time a friend of a friend becomes, if not a cherished companion, then at least a friendly acquaintance.

Most of the time the family of your friend becomes, if not your own extended family, at least a group of people you can love for her sake.

Most of the time, when our circles of love intersect, there's simply more love to go around.

And in this world where so many people feel friendless and uncared-for, more love can't help but be a good thing.

A Friendship Story

"A group of 25 girls began a club in 1929 which has lasted to 1999 and beyond. There are 17 women left in this group and the Lord has had His hand on each of our lives. There was a prayer we would all say together at our meetings. We have shared our lives about dates, engagements, weddings, baby showers, and now the third generation are sometimes at our gatherings. Our husbands have been associated with our group for many years so we wouldn't be driving long distances alone. Philanthropic work was done in the earlier years and our mothers were honored each year. Many in the group have traveled extensively and we have all benefited from this. The original group did not smoke or drink and there were no divorces in the group. Many women have lost their husbands, two doctors and a judge among them. Eight couples in the group have had 50 or more years together. It has been an unusual friendship over these many years."

—Roie Alys Underhill,
Hemet, California

33 Fun and Fruitful Ideas for Being Together

1. Read a book aloud—or start a "circle of friends" book club.
2. Do all your cooking for a week in double batches, then freeze them.
3. Pack a lunch in backpacks and take a *long* walk.
4. Make an appointment for two at a day spa. Get facials, massage, manicures—whatever makes you feel most pampered and beautiful.
5. Spend an autumn afternoon planting bulbs together.
6. Learn to make stained glass.
7. Pray together.
8. Expand your understanding by attending a service of a different denomination or faith.
9. Team up on big chores like organizing the pantry or painting the bedrooms.
10. Drive to a nearby small town and have lunch in a little place where you've never been before.
11. Meet in another city for a weekend.
12. Rent a movie and gather both families together to watch it.
13. Celebrate a holiday together.
14. Sing or play a duet on piano, guitar, or kazoo.
15. Work together on a service project: serving at a soup line, repairing houses for the elderly, reading stories to children.
16. Cook a meal for a shut-in friend and deliver it together.
17. Team-teach a class at your local hobby store, university extension, or neighborhood center.
18. Cross-stitch matching pillows for your sofas.

19. Schedule a "put in album" day for all those photos that have piled up.

20. On *another* day, spend the afternoon thumbing through albums and looking at photos of each other from grade school, high school, and college. You may laugh, but kindly!

21. Rent or borrow a video camera if you don't own one and shoot videos of each other's families.

22. Have a "friends of friends" party. Ask each guest to bring a guest the others probably don't know. Have fun meeting people from many different walks of life and actively expand your circles of love.

23. Spend your lunch hour at the skating rink.

24. Buy or make kites and take them to the park to fly. (If the kids are good, they can come along.)

25. Set up two ironing boards, pop a great CD in the player, and take care of all your "pressing" concerns.

26. Get tough. Go shopping!

27. Make a date to attend the "twilight" matinee— usually the least expensive showing, around 4:30 P.M.—of the newest "chick flick" in town. Bring lots of tissues.

28. Have breakfast together early on a Friday or Saturday and then go garage-sale hopping. Bring a newspaper, a local map, and some cash (many sales don't take checks).

29. Play a game of Monopoly or Scrabble.

30. Plan a party for your other friends.

31. Refinish old furniture together.

32. Give each other a back rub or a foot rub . . . or both!

33. Write a book together!

Just Being

Just recently we spent the weekend together at Emilie's house. And it was wonderful!

We didn't work.

We didn't go out to shop or see a movie.

We didn't get together with other friends.

Sometimes we didn't even talk.

We simply enjoyed being with each other.

We read a little.

We took a nap.

We reminisced quietly.

We prayed.

What a sweet, precious time of being together, rejoicing in the warmth and security of knowing you're with someone who loves to be with you.

That's something to remember always, when you're spending time with a friend of the heart.

Play together.

Work together.

Share your spirits.

Share the people in your life.

But make sure there's some time left over just to be . . . together.

Something to ponder . . .

*Here's something I want to do with
my friend this week . . .*

The ABC's of Friendship

We didn't invent this one, but we love it!

A Friend . . .

Accepts you as you are.
Believes in you.
Calls you just to say "hi."
Doesn't give up on you.
Envisions the whole of you, even the unfinished parts.
Forgives your mistakes.
Gives unconditionally.
Helps you.
Invites you over to
Just "be" with you.
Keeps you close at heart.
Loves you for who you are.
Makes a difference in your life.
Never judges.
Offers support.
Picks you up.
Quiets your fears.
Raises your spirits.
Says nice things about you.
Tells you the truth when you need to hear it.
Understands you.
Values you.
Walks beside you.
X-plains things you don't understand.
Yells when you won't listen and
Zaps you back to reality!

—Author unknown

*"Friendship," said
Christopher Robin,
"is a very comforting
sort of thing to have."*

—A. A. MILNE

4

"You Make Me Feel Loved"

The Care and Maintenance of Treasured Friends

Whatever you yourself desire, I will do it for you.
—THE BOOK OF FIRST SAMUEL

Like a Garden

We're not the first people to observe that friendship is like a garden. But we love to think of it that way, because we like to think of our relationships as lovely, leafy, growing, life-giving.

And, of course, that reminds us that friendships, like gardens, need care.

Yes, you can plant a seed and let it take care of itself, and something probably will grow.

But you get the best results with a lot of watering and fertilizing and weeding and nurturing.

Besides, caring for each other is one of the basic purposes of friendship. We all need the encouragement, the understanding, the advocacy that a friendship brings us. We all need the reassurance that we are worth some trouble.

And here's something else: In a sense, it's the very act of caring for our friendships that make them so precious to us. We tend to love those things in which we've invested our time, our energies, our money, our efforts. As the poet Ezra Pound put it, "What thou lov'st well is thy true heritage."

That's one reason we love our well-tended gardens—not just for the fruits and the flowers, but also for the pruning, the spraying, the pulling, for the investments of seed and fertilizer, even for the sunburn and the blisters.

We love best those things (and those people) in which we have invested acts of love.

Even better, we love those things (and those people) in which the investment of love is a mutual thing.

Two gardens can't care for each other.

But two people can.

And that, to an important degree, is what friends are for.

Everyday Maintenance

How do you take care of a friendship?

A lot of it just comes naturally. As you spend time together and enjoy each other and help each other, chances are you're also taking care of each other and nurturing your friendship. And yet, like any other worthwhile relationships, friendship blossoms most beautifully with the investment of a little deliberate care and nurturing.

Most of the time, a little everyday maintenance is all you need to keep a friendship growing. A phone call. An e-mail. A quick note scrawled at the bottom of a funny card and dropped in the mailbox. A touch on the arm or a hug in passing. A quick visit and a chat and a promise to get together again soon. A thoughtful gift. A silly surprise.

Years ago, when Donna had decided to whip her nonathletic body in shape and had finally dared her first 10K race, a good friend met her at the finish line and plopped a laurel wreath on her panting, perspiring head.

More recently, Emilie's good friend Barbara surprised her with the gift of antique tea towels inscribed with "sister." (Then Emilie had a set embroidered for Donna!)

All of our friends love to send cards back and forth, to scribble notes on the backs of photographs and pop them in envelopes. We love to collect little remembrances from antique shops or even toy stores and give them to our friends, or to cook up special recipes of goodies to share. We love to pick up the phone and share a cup of tea together while we chat.

And it is these little gifts and gestures between friends that help keep us connected, that comfort and encourage us, that remind us of how much we care and are cared for.

Faithfulness in little things helps, too. You are caring for your friendship when you show up for your coffee date, when you think twice about canceling your walk together, when you make a note to pray for your friend—then read the note and actually do it. Kept promises fertilize a friendship.

And just as weeding is part of caring for a garden, addressing the problems between you is a vital part of everyday friendship maintenance. In even the best friendships you will encounter petty annoyances, minor hurts, feelings of neglect and distance.

Your friend is too busy one week to call you.

Or you show up consistently late for your lunch dates.

Or one of you suspects the other of breaking a confidence.

Or you simply exchange sharp words on a bad day.

Like weeds, negative feelings between friends can grow if left untended. They have even been known to choke a friendship. So the thing to do when problems occur is to take care of them while they are fresh and small.

And notice: Taking care of problems does not always require a confrontation. It doesn't always even call for a conversation. Sometimes you will simply choose to recognize and dismiss the problem. You will say to yourself, "Oh, she's just stressed out," or "She's just too snowed-under to call," or "That's just the way she is."

And then you realize that you really do trust your friend's love. You understand why the problem happened. You *love* her just the way she is. You're willing to let the matter slide, to put the hurt behind you.

That really is a valid way to handle some problems between friends.

But be careful. Because letting a matter slide can also be a way to avoid resolving issues. And when you fail to resolve real issues, you allow a distance to grow between you.

Unresolved anger, feelings of betrayal, feelings of hurt—these can easily choke out a friendship.

When in doubt, then, it's better to talk. Sometimes nurturing a friendship means gently confronting your friend. It means confessing your feelings of hurt or anger. It means swallowing your pride and apologizing . . . or opening your heart to forgive. It means saying again these words: "You matter to me. I don't want to hurt you. You are worth so much more to me than my hurt feelings and my pride."

Taking care of problems—that's just a part of everyday business in any relationship, friendships included. And it's better done sooner than later.

Most of all, everyday maintenance is a matter of keeping each other in mind, even when you can't get together.

It means remembering why a particular day is special . . . or hard . . . and making a point to find out how it went.

It means knowing what is going on with each other's family and work, and keeping up with what's new.

It means checking in on a regular basis, just to know that everything's going all right.

It means doing what you can, when you can, to make your friend feel loved.

These are the everyday connections that nurture friendship. They are the little reminders that say: "Yes, I'm still here. I know you're there, too. Never, ever forget that I care about you."

That kind of everyday maintenance doesn't actually have to take place every day. How often you touch base will depend a lot on where you live, what you do, what your expectations for each other are.

And it doesn't really involve much time or energy or money—but it requires some. It's just a matter of paying attention, of giving your friendship some priority, of reminding yourself that friendship is not a luxury and that friendships can't thrive without a little attention. When you are parceling out the pieces of yourself, it's important to reserve a chunk for the friends of your heart.

For ordinary, everyday care of a relationship, think *little things—regularly and often.*

Think contact and constancy, watering and weeding.

Then think . . . daisies and gardenias, avocados and artichokes—a flowering, fragrant garden of love and delight.

A well-nourished, well-cultivated friendship of the heart.

Extravagance

*N*ot all gestures of friendship are little, of course.

Friends of the heart not only love daily and faithfully; they also know how to love extravagantly when extravagance is appropriate.

When your friend is in need, it's appropriate to do everything you can to *be* there, to help. Even if it means taking a day off work. Even if it means giving up your weekends or driving hundreds of miles. Even (and this is hard!) if it means giving up her attention so that she can get some much needed rest. . . .

When your friend celebrates a milestone—a wedding, a graduation, the opening of a new business, or the start of a new phase in life—it's appropriate to splurge on something very special. Even if it means organizing an extravagant reunion. Even if it means traveling out of town and shopping for hours to find just the perfect gift. Even if it means months and months of needlework to finish a handmade gift or hours and hours at the computer putting together just the perfect written tribute.

When you have been friends for a while and you want to express just how much she means to you, it's appropriate to pull out all the stops (in terms of finance or of time or of effort) to give her just the perfect gift or find the perfect words to say what you really feel. Even if it means spending a little more than you can afford or going to more shops than you have time to visit or planning far in advance or staying up half the night.

You see, thrift is a good thing.

Prudence is a good thing.

Wisdom is definitely a good thing. And it's wise to count the cost of relationship, to set your boundaries in terms of how much time and effort and money you can afford to invest in any given relationship.

But when it comes to friends of your heart, it's also a good thing sometimes to throw caution to the wind and give beyond what is thrifty. Beyond what is prudent. Beyond what some people might think is wise.

Thus, we know women who have given away a cherished family heirloom to a treasured friend: their mother's ring, a beloved painting or book, a carefully guarded piece of antique porcelain. Donna's friend Anne Johnson once made Donna cry over the gift of her grandmother's special cranberry dish—and the thought of that loving gift can still bring tears to Donna's eyes.

We know women who have flown cross-country to support a friend during a time of family crisis and have stayed for weeks, helping with the driving and the laundry and the meals, helping their friends go on when the way was difficult.

We know women who have listened for hours while their bereaved friends talked through their grief again and again . . . or have given up weekends to baby-sit . . . or have offered their sofas and their extra rooms for days or weeks or months . . . or have helped nurse their friend's elderly parents . . . or have even walked with friends into the valley of the shadow of death.

Jesus of Nazareth once said, "Greater love has no one than this, than to lay down one's life for his friends." But laying down one's life for someone doesn't necessarily mean literally dying for them. What it does mean is willing and joyful sacrifice—of your time, of your freedom, of your ease, of your financial resources and your prized possessions. It means the generous, unthrifty, imprudent giving of yourself to someone you love. To your friend.

Now, you wouldn't do it for everyone.

You wouldn't do it all of the time for anyone.

But for your special, well-loved friend of the heart, an act of sacrifice can be a lovely and beautiful gesture. It can bring surprising joy to both giver and recipient. It can bring the two of you closer than you've ever been.

And yes, there are pitfalls to beware when it comes to extravagant giving. The giver must watch her motives, being sure that her giving is not a form of manipulation, a guilt-lever or bribe. It must not be an attempt to win friendship or to shore up one's own feelings of insecurity. It must not feel like charity or one-upmanship.

Even an extravagant, sacrificial gift, in other words, must be just that—a gift. The only strings attached must be heartstrings.

For the recipient, the primary pitfall is pride and discomfort. It can feel strange to be the recipient of generous, heartfelt, over-the-top giving. The challenge is to accept the sacrifice with gratitude and humility, to return the love without feeling the need to top the gift.

And all this means that prudence and wisdom do enter into the situation after all.

It really is important to count the cost of going all out, to weigh the risks and ponder the consequences.

But just as important sometimes is to decide a friend is worth whatever it takes.

And it's true.

A true friend of the heart is worth almost anything you choose to give.

A Double Friendship Story

"I met my friend Marina Papineau through my daughter's friendship with her son. Our children were 'sweethearts' at the time of their eighth grade graduation in 1995. It was at that reception that Marina asked me, 'Will we still be friends if our kids break up?' My response was, 'I'm not your friend because of our children. . . . Our friendship's foundation is strong and the only thing that will change is for our friendship to become stronger.'

"Marina and I have been friends now for more than five years. Whenever we are together it's as though we are schoolgirls. We both love 'tea time,' and that is what really made our friendship. We try new tearooms on occasion, or one will invite the other into our home for that 'special' time together. I call Marina my 'teapot' friend, because she *always* knows when my cup needs to be filled with that refreshing flavor of love. . . .

"We have regular activities we do together annually. At Christmas we attend a different activity each year: a ballet, symphony, children's choir, craft fairs at each season, but our favorite spot several times a year is having lunch at Hellos, our favorite tearoom. I look forward to the years in which we grow old 'gracefully' together. And I'm very certain this friendship will last for eternity, because our heavenly Father is preparing a 'tearoom' for us."

—Dawn Beaty,
Westfield, Indiana

"It is hard to say the precise moment my friendship started with my close friend, Dawn Beaty. My son and her daughter had started liking each other in junior high. (They are both seniors now.) We knew who each other was as we lived just down the street from each other. Somehow, we both decided to take our daughters to our favorite tea room, Hellos, before school started. We so enjoyed the day that this has become a yearly outing with our daughters. . . .

"I always look forward to our outings. The time we spend together just flies by. There are times where I feel like I have neglected her with my hectic schedule. I just call Dawn and say we must get together, I need my cup filled with her love and friendship. We do so much together. We have been to several tearooms, the ballet, the symphony, shopping at craft fairs, our children's sporting events, and for the first time a weekend trip to a bed and breakfast. Each Christmas we take a day for ourselves and plan something we have not done before. It is so exciting to plan our outing and then to just relax and enjoy it. . . .

"I know that she has filled my cup to overflowing so many times. It could just be a card, a wave as she drives by, or just five minutes on the phone and I feel my heart bursting. I can always walk away and know that I am smiling all the way home. She is always there willing to listen and help out. . . . As I talk to the Lord, I always make sure I tell Him thank you for sending her to me. He knows how much I need her."

—Marina Papineau,
Westfield, Indiana

In Short: A Summary of Friendship Maintenance

It's the little, thoughtful touches that keep your garden growing.

It's the big, extravagant, over-the-top gestures that twine your hearts together forever.

Think: A daisy a day . . . and sometimes a roomful of roses.

Something to ponder. . .

*If I could give my friend anything
in the world, it would be . . .*

Again, God's Word calls us to test the spirits behind the teaching we hear to be sure that we are indeed learning His truth.

Beware of Deceiving Spirits

In addition to warning us against self-deception and false prophets and teachers, the Bible warns us against the deception that comes through demonic influence.

- Dave tells us about Ashley, whom he met at a junior-high camp.

  — What did Ashley learn from Luke 16:19-26, especially verse 26?

  — What did you learn about Satan's strategies from Ashley's experience?

- Look again at the kind of prayer we need to pray in order to keep ourselves from deceiving spirits (page 175 in the text). In a few quiet moments of prayer now, let these words be your own. Ask God to open your eyes to any deception you may have accepted as truth.

Spiritual Discernment

Our first line of defense against Satan's deception is discernment—the act of judging whether something is right or wrong so that the right can be accepted and the wrong discarded.

- Discernment is the buzzer that sounds inside you, warning that something is wrong. And discernment is an act of the Holy Spirit, who dwells within us.

— Why is discernment an important gift to individual believers and to the church in general?

— When has the Holy Spirit helped you recognize wrong and resist or discard it? Be specific.

• Why are we more vulnerable to Satan's deception than to his temptations or accusations?

• What is the only effective weapon against the darkness of Satan's deception? (See John 8:31,32 and John 17:17.)

The light of God's truth, as revealed in His Word, is the only effective weapon against the darkness of deception. Know His Word so that you can wield it effectively against the deceiver.

A Step Toward Freedom

- This chapter may have given you a greater appreciation for the value of Bible study. What step will you take to strengthen your Bible study program so that you can be better equipped to see through Satan's deceptions? Be specific in your plan and realistic in your goals. It's always a good idea to have someone hold you accountable—and it's ideal to work with a partner.

- Thank God for the protection and wisdom available to you as His child. Thank Him, too, for His Spirit, who dwells within you and gives you the gift of discernment. Then ask the Holy Spirit to help you as you consider each of the areas of self-deception that Satan can use to his advantage and your disadvantage. Ask God's Spirit to help you discern where you may be deceiving yourself...and ask the Spirit to help you recognize any false teachers you may be influenced by...as well as any deceiving spirits at work in your life. Finally, thank God for His Word and ask Him to be with you as you seek to know Him better through the Scriptures.

The Danger of
Losing Control

TWELVE

Satan's Influence

- What did you learn from Sheila's experience about how Satan works?

- According to 1 Peter 1:17-19 and Romans 8:35-39, why does demonic *bondage* never mean satanic *ownership*?

Although it may not be easy to admit, we Christians can lose our freedom and can surrender to demonic influences. There is much clear evidence in Scripture that believers who repeatedly give in to temptation, accusation, and deception can fall into bondage.

Saints in Bondage

Since we live in a world whose god is Satan, the possibility of being tempted, deceived, and accused is constant. If we allow Satan's schemes to influence us, we can lose control to the degree that we have been deceived.

- It is important to understand that Christians are targets for demonic influence.

  — What two options are we left with if we don't acknowledge the very real activity of demons in this world?

  — What thinking do these two options lead to? In other words, what are the consequences of blaming ourselves for the problems we face? Of blaming God?

We are in a winnable war against demonic powers. But, as we've said a number of times, if Satan can get you to believe a lie, he can control your life.

- The New Testament offers examples as well as teachings that reflect the truth that believers can come under bondage to demonic influence.

  — *Luke 13:10-17.* Where was the woman Jesus healed (verse 10)? How was she described (verse 16)? What things didn't protect her from Satan's power?

  —*Luke 22:31-34.* What request did Satan make of Jesus? And what does the fact that this request was made suggest about a believer's vulnerability?

  — *Ephesians 6:10-17.* What does the existence of the armor Paul describes here and the command to put it on suggest about the power and strategy of demons? About your vulnerability?

— *James 3:14-16.* What does James warn believers about here?

— *1 Timothy 4:1-3.* Who will be "paying attention to deceitful spirits and doctrines of demons"? What warning is implied in this statement?

— *1 Corinthians 5:1-13.* Paul hoped that the man referred to in this passage would experience the natural consequences of his sin, repent, and be set free from his bondage. What clue in this passage suggests that the man was a believer? When have the natural consequences of your sin moved you to repent?

— *Ephesians 4:26,27.* According to this passage, what is one way we believers can give Satan a foothold in our lives? Are you nursing any anger, bitterness, or unforgiveness? If so, Satan has a place in your life from which to work.

— *1 Peter 5:6-9.* What are two more ways that we believers can give Satan a foothold in our life? Also, notice how Peter talks about the devil here. What does the image suggest to you?

— *Acts 5:1-11*. What does the story of Ananias and Sapphira teach you about the importance of truth? What does their story teach about the possibility and consequences of Satan's control of believers?

It is possible for believers—for you and for me—to be filled either with satanic deception or the Spirit of God. To whichever source we yield, by that source we shall be filled and controlled.

The Devil Did Not Make You Do It!

When, like Ananias and Sapphira, you open the door of your life to Satan, he will take full advantage of the opportunity.

• Consider again the story of Ananias and Sapphira.

    — Read Peter's questions to them in Acts 5:4,9. What do you think prompted them to lie about the income they received from the sale of their land?

    — What is inaccurate about the statement, "The devil made me do it"? How is a person's freedom to make choices involved in the devil's control of his or her life?

When we fail to resist temptation, accusation, or deception, Satan will enter our life. If we continue to allow him access to that area, he will eventually control it. We won't lose our salvation, but we will lose our daily victory.

    — Despite this truth, many young Christians who cannot control some area of their life blame themselves instead of dealing with the problem. How might Satan be involved in this?

— An area of bondage is anything bad you cannot stop doing and anything good you cannot make yourself do. According to this definition, what areas of bondage—if any—exist in your life today? If there are any areas, what will you do to resist Satan? Who will you go to for support?

We have all the resources and protection we need to live a victorious life in Christ every day. If we're not living it, it's our choice.

If We're Not Responsible, We Will Lose Control

• God's protection depends on our willingness to apply the protection He has provided.

— According to the following passages, what must you do to experience God's protection?

Romans 13:14

James 4:7

Ephesians 6:10-17

Romans 6:12

Choosing truth, living a righteous life, and putting on the armor of God is each believer's individual responsibility. If you go into battle without your armor, you may get hurt—and you alone are responsible for putting on that armor. You alone make such choices for yourself, choices to protect yourself from Satan by not giving him a foothold in your life.

A Step Toward Freedom

- Read what Paul says in Romans 7:15. What about yourself—if anything—do his words remind you of? If you yourself could have written these words today, let the prayer below guide you through a time of confession. If you aren't struggling right now, thank God and ask Him to protect you from being proud of that fact, for pride can serve as a foothold for Satan.

- Knowing that the apostle Paul himself struggled with doing the very thing he hated, confess to God where you have been doing exactly what you hate...confess where you now see that you were a target for Satan's temptation, accusation, and deception. If you're not sure, ask God to help you see yourself as He sees you: as you really are. Having recognized Satan's activity in your life, now confess how you gave him a foothold in your life...and renounce your involvement with him. Finally, thank God for the gift of His Son, Jesus Christ the Bondage Breaker, and for the freedom that is available to you in Him.

Part 3

Walk Free!

Steps to Freedom in Christ

THIRTEEN

Taking Inventory

If you have received Christ as your personal Savior, He has set you free from sin and Satan's power through His victory on the cross and His resurrection. But if you are not experiencing freedom in your daily life, it may be because you have not realized who you are in Christ and taken a stand against the devil and his lies.

- In what areas of your life, if any, are you not experiencing freedom?

Now you can begin working through the following seven steps toward full freedom and victory in Christ. Again, keep in mind that no one can take these steps for you.

- As you take these steps, who will be walking this path with you? Who will be praying for you? What mature Christian will be helping you and encouraging you each step of the way?

The battle for your mind can only be won as you personally choose truth. Know that you can win this battle with the protection God has provided for you in Christ!

An Opening Prayer

- As you begin, you may find yourself thinking, "This isn't going to work" or "God doesn't love me."

    — Who is the source of thoughts like these?

    — What will you do to defend yourself against them?

Satan's lies can stop you only if you believe them. Uncover the lie and Satan's power is broken.

- Explain why you must speak out loud when you uncover Satan's lies and want to confront him.

- Now pray aloud the following prayer:

    Dear heavenly Father, I know that You are here in this room and present in my life. You are the only all-knowing, all-powerful, ever-present God. I desperately need You because without Jesus I can do nothing.

    I believe the Bible because it tells me what is really true. I refuse to believe the lies of Satan. I stand in the truth that all authority in heaven and on earth has been given to the risen Christ. I ask You to protect my thoughts and mind, to fill me with Your Holy Spirit, and to lead me into all

> *truth. I pray for Your complete protection. In Jesus'*
> *name I pray, amen.*

Then have your Christian friend or counselor declare aloud these truths:

> *In the name and the authority of the Lord Jesus*
> *Christ, we command Satan and all evil spirits to*
> *let go of (name) in order that (name) can be free*
> *to know and choose to do the will of God. As chil-*
> *dren of God seated with Christ in the heavenlies,*
> *we agree that every enemy of the Lord Jesus Christ*
> *be bound and gagged to silence in (name). We say*
> *to Satan and all of his evil workers that you cannot*
> *inflict any pain or in any way stop or hinder God's*
> *will from being done today in (name).*

Having commanded Satan and his evil workers to leave you alone, you can now begin working on these seven steps.

Step 1: Counterfeit vs. Real

The first step to freedom in Christ is to turn your back on any present or past involvement with satanically inspired occult practices or false religions.

- Pray aloud the following prayer:

> *Dear heavenly Father, I ask You to reveal to me*
> *anything that I have done or that someone has*
> *done to me that is spiritually wrong. Show me how*
> *I have been involved with any cults, false religions,*
> *occult/satanic practices, or false teachers, whether*
> *I knew I was involved or not. I want to experience*
> *Your freedom and do Your will. I ask this in Jesus'*
> *name, amen.*

- Complete, if you haven't already, the "Non-Christian Spiritual Checklist" found on pages 196–197 of the text.

- Now list the titles of anti-Christian movies, music, books, magazines, comic books, TV programs, video games, Internet sites, and anything else that may have influenced you in a wrong way.

- Answer the following six questions:
  — Have you ever felt, heard, or seen a spiritual being in your room?

  — Have you had an imaginary friend who talks to you?

  — Have you ever heard voices in your head or had repeating, nagging thoughts like, "I'm dumb," "I'm ugly," "I can't do anything right," and so on, as if there were a conversation going on in your head?

  — Have you or has anyone in your family ever consulted a medium, spiritist, or channeler?

  — What other spiritual experiences have you had that could be considered out of the ordinary (telepathy, speaking in a trance, knowing something supernaturally, and so on)?

— Have you ever been involved in satanic worship of any form or attended a concert where Satan was the focus?

- Then, as you were directed in the text, pray the following prayer for each item on your list:

> *Lord, I confess that I have participated in _____. I know it was wrong and offensive in Your sight. Thank You for Your forgiveness. I renounce any and all involvement with _____ because it is a counterfeit to true Christianity, and I cancel out any and all ground that the enemy has gained in my life through this activity. In Jesus' name, amen.*

To experience true freedom in Christ, you must renounce all contact with cults, false religions, occult/satanic practices, and false teachers as the Lord allows you to remember them. You must recognize that they are counterfeits to true Christianity.

Renouncing Wrong Priorities

Confront your wrong priorities—those areas where things or people have become more important to you than the true God, Jesus Christ.

- Who were we created to worship?

- What can idols be, besides stone or wooden images?

- If you haven't already done it, complete the checklist on page 200 of the text.

- Use the following prayer to renounce any areas of idolatry or wrong priority the Holy Spirit brings to your mind.

> *In the name of the true and living God, Jesus Christ, I renounce my worship of the false god of (name the idol). I choose to worship only You, Lord. I ask You, Father, to enable me to keep this area of (name the idol) in its proper place in my life.*

Satanic Ritual Involvement

Have you been involved in satanic rituals or heavy occult activity? Or have you experienced severe nightmares, suggesting that satanic, occult activity in your past has been blocked from your memory?

- Specifically renounce all satanic rituals, covenants (promises), and assignments as the Lord allows you to remember them.

Step 2: Deception vs. Truth

Second, you must choose God's truth and get rid of anything false in your life (Ephesians 4:15,25).

- Begin this important step by reading aloud the following prayer:

> *Dear heavenly Father, I know that You want me to face the truth and that I must be honest with You. I know that choosing to believe the truth will set me free. I have been deceived by Satan, the father of lies, and I have deceived myself. I thought I could hide it from You, but You see everything and still love me.*
>
> *I pray in the name of the Lord Jesus Christ, asking You to rebuke all of Satan's demons through Your righteous Son Jesus, who shed His blood on the cross and rose from the dead for me. I have asked Jesus into my life, and I am Your child. Therefore, by the authority of the Lord Jesus Christ, I command all evil spirits to leave me. I ask the Holy Spirit to lead me into all truth.*

I ask You to look deep inside me and know my heart. Show me if there is anything in me that I am trying to hide, because I want to be free. In Jesus' name I pray, amen.

(See John 8:32; 8:44; 1 John 1:8; Psalm 139:23,24)

- Now think about the evil tricks Satan has used to deceive you into relying on yourself, rather than trusting in your Father in heaven.

Ways You Can Be Deceived by the World

- Work through the checklist on pages 202–203 of the text and list the areas that apply to your life.

- Pray this prayer of confession for each item you check:

  Lord, I confess that I have been deceived by _____. I thank You for Your forgiveness, and I commit myself to believing only Your truth. In Jesus' name, amen.

Ways You Can Deceive Yourself

- Complete the checklist on pages 203–204 of the text.

- Pray this prayer of confession for each self-deception you need to renounce:

  Lord, I confess that I have deceived myself by _____. Thank You for Your forgiveness. I commit myself to believing only Your truth. In Jesus' name, amen.

Wrong Ways to Defend Yourself

- Complete the checklist on page 204 of the text. Depend on God to help you put down the things that are necessary for you to confess.

- Use this prayer to confess aloud each of these sins:

    Lord, I confess that I have defended myself wrongly by _____. Thank You for Your forgiveness. I now commit myself to trusting in You to defend and protect me. In Jesus' name, amen.

- What do we need to learn about the lies we have used to defend ourselves?

Ways That We Can Be Deceived About God

We must believe what God says, especially what He says about *Himself.*

- What must we recognize about faith?

- If you have found that your relationship with God the Father is hurt by your past experiences, read your way *out loud* through the lists on page 206 of the text ("I renounce the lie..."; "I joyfully accept the truth...").

Ways That Our Fears Deceive Us

A central part of walking in the truth and rejecting deception is to deal with the fears that harass us. Fear weakens us, causes us to be self-centered, and clouds our minds. But it can only control us if we let it.

- In order to begin to experience freedom from the bondage of fear and the ability to walk by faith in God, pray the following prayer from your heart:

> *Dear heavenly Father, I confess to You that I have listened to the devil's roar and have allowed fear to master me. I have not always walked by faith in You but instead have focused on my feelings and circumstances. Thank You for forgiving me for my unbelief.*
>
> *Right now I renounce the spirit of fear and affirm the truth that You have not given me a spirit of fear but of power, love, and a sound mind. Lord, please reveal to my mind now all the fears that have been controlling me so I can renounce them and be free to walk by faith in You.*
>
> *I thank You for the freedom You give me to walk by faith and not by fear. In Jesus' powerful name, I pray, amen.*
>
> (SEE 2 CORINTHIANS 4:16-18; 5:7; 2 TIMOTHY 1:7)

- Use the checklist on page 208 of the text as a guide to identifying fears in your life. Write down as many areas as God enables you to.

- Follow this by renouncing each fear specifically, using this prayer:

> *I renounce the (<u>name the fear</u>) because God has not given me a spirit of fear. I choose to live by faith in the God who has promised to protect me and meet all my needs as I walk by faith in Him.*
>
> (SEE PSALM 27:1; MATTHEW 6:33,34; 2 TIMOTHY 1:7)

- Finish up your dealing with fear by praying this:

> *Dear heavenly Father, I thank You that You are trustworthy. I choose to believe You, even when my feelings and circumstances tell me to fear. You have told me not to fear, for You are with me; to not anxiously look about me, for You are my God. You will strengthen me, help me, and surely uphold me with Your righteous right hand. I pray this with faith in the name of Jesus my Master, amen.*
>
> (SEE ISAIAH 41:10)

Faith Must Be Based on the Truth of God's Word

Fear stands opposed to faith, and real faith must be grounded in the truth.

- How has the New Age movement twisted the idea of faith?

- Why must our faith be based on God and His Word?

- Choosing truth may be difficult if you have been living a lie (been deceived) for some time. Filling your mind and heart with the truth is the best way to free yourself from deception.

— Read aloud the following "Statement of Truth."

1. I believe that there is only one true and living God (Exodus 20:2,3), who exists as the Father, Son, and Holy Spirit. He alone is worthy of all honor, praise, and glory. I believe that He made all things and holds all things together (Colossians 1:16,17).

2. I recognize Jesus Christ as the Messiah, the Word who became flesh and lived with us (John 1:1,14). I believe that He came to destroy the works of Satan (1 John 3:8).

3. I believe that God showed how much He loves me by sending Christ to die for me, even though I was sinful (Romans 5:8). I believe that God rescued me from the kingdom of darkness and brought me into the kingdom of His Son, who has forgiven my sins and set me free (Colossians 1:13,14).

4. I believe I am spiritually strong because Jesus is my strength. I have the authority to stand against Satan because I am a child of God (1 John 3:1-3). I believe that I was saved by the grace of God through faith, that it was a gift and not the result of any works on my part (Ephesians 2:8).

5. I choose to be strong in the Lord and in the strength of His might (Ephesians 6:10). I put no confidence in the flesh (Philippians 3:3), for the weapons of our warfare are not of the flesh (2 Corinthians 10:4). I put on the whole armor of God (Ephesians 6:10-17), and I resolve to stand firm in my faith and resist the evil one.

6. I believe that apart from Christ I can do nothing (John 15:5), so I will depend totally on Him. I choose to remain in Christ in order to bear much fruit and glorify the Lord (John 15:8). I announce to Satan that Jesus is my Lord (1 Corinthians 12:3), and I reject any counterfeit gifts or works of Satan in my life.

7. I believe that the truth will set me free (John 8:32). I stand against Satan's lies by taking every thought captive in obedience to Christ (2 Corinthians 10:5). I believe that the Bible is the only reliable guide for my life (2 Timothy 3:15,16). I choose to speak the truth in love (Ephesians 4:15).

8. I choose to give my body to God to be used for righteousness, a living and holy sacrifice, and I choose to renew my mind by God's Word (Romans 6:13; 12:1,2). I have put off the old self with its evil practices and have put on the new self (Colossians 3:9,10). I am a new creature in Christ (2 Corinthians 5:17).

9. I ask my heavenly Father to fill me with His Holy Spirit (Ephesians 5:18), to lead me into all truth (John 16:13), and to give me

power to live above sin and not carry out the desires of the flesh (Galatians 5:16). I crucify the flesh and choose to be led by and obey the Holy Spirit (Galatians 5:24,25).

10. I renounce all selfish goals and choose the ultimate goal of love (1 Timothy 1:5). I choose to obey the two greatest commandments: to love the Lord my God with all my heart, soul, and mind, and to love others in the same way I love myself (Matthew 22:37-39).

11. I believe that Jesus has all authority in heaven and on earth (Matthew 28:18) and that He rules over everything (Colossians 2:10). I believe that Satan and his demons are subject to me in Christ because I am a member of His body (Ephesians 1:19-23). I will obey God's command to submit to Him and to resist the devil (James 4:7). I command Satan in the name of Christ to leave my presence.

- What questions, if any, do you have about what you've read? Get answers from a more mature Christian (perhaps a pastor or youth leader) so that you can read these words of truth with conviction.

Read the Statement of Truth every day for several weeks in order to renew your mind and build your faith. After all, that's what God's truth is designed to do.

Step 3: Bitterness vs. Forgiveness

If you do not forgive people who hurt you or offend you, you are a wide-open target for Satan's attacks. You need to forgive others so that Satan can't take advantage of you (2 Corinthians 2:10,11).

- Ask God to bring to mind those people you need to forgive as you read the prayer below. Make a list of those names.

Dear heavenly Father, thank You for Your kindness and patience that led me to turn from my sin. I have not always been kind, patient, and loving toward others, especially those who have hurt me.

*I have been bitter and resentful. I give You my
emotions, and ask You to bring to the surface all
my painful memories so I can choose to forgive
from my heart. I ask You to bring to my mind the
people I need to forgive. I ask this in the precious
name of Jesus, who will heal me from my hurts,
amen.*

(SEE ROMANS 2:4; MATTHEW 18:35)

- Did your name appear on the list? Did you list God? What do
  you need to forgive yourself for? What anger toward God do
  you need to confess?

- Now review the discussion of forgiveness (pages 212–214
  in the text).

    — What ideas about forgiveness are new to you?

    — What encouragement did you find in this discussion?
      What conviction?

- Having been nudged by the Holy Spirit, choose to forgive the
  people on your list. Don't wait to forgive until you feel like
  forgiving. (You'll never get there.) Forgive those who have
  hurt you by praying aloud,

    *Lord, I forgive (name) for (specifically name all of
    his/her offenses and your painful memories).*

Remember that you forgive someone for *your* sake so that *you* can
be free. Your need to forgive isn't an issue between you and the
person who hurt you; it's between you and God.

Step 4: Rebellion vs. Submission

The Bible teaches that we have two responsibilities to the human authorities God has placed over us: to pray for them and to submit to them. Disobeying God's commands and rebelling against God, your parents, and other authorities gives Satan an opportunity to attack.

- Explain why being submissive to parents, teachers, and the government demonstrates your faith in God.

- Under what circumstances does God permit us to disobey earthly leaders? The Bible is very specific.

- If you have questions about how God wants you to respond to authorities in your life, talk to your pastor or youth leader or open the Bible to some of the passages listed on page 215 of the text.

- To begin Step 4, pray aloud the following prayer:

    Dear heavenly Father, You have said in the Bible that rebellion is as bad as witchcraft and disobedience as sinful as serving false gods. I know that I have disobeyed You by rebelling in my heart against You and against those people You have put in authority over me. I ask Your forgiveness for my rebellion.

    By the shed blood of the Lord Jesus Christ, I resist all evil spirits that took advantage of my rebellion. I pray that You will show me all the ways

I have been rebellious. I choose to adopt a submissive spirit and servant's heart. In the name of Jesus Christ my Lord, amen.

(SEE 1 SAMUEL 15:23)

• As you prayerfully look over the checklist on page 216 of the text, allow the Lord to show you any *specific* ways in which you have been rebellious to authority. For each way the Spirit of God brings to mind that you have been rebellious, use the following prayer to confess that sin:

Lord, I confess that I have been rebellious toward (name) by (say what you did specifically). Thank You for forgiving my rebellion. I choose now to be submissive and obedient to Your Word. In Jesus' name I pray, amen.

When we submit to God's line of authority, we are choosing to believe that God will protect and bless us.

Step 5: Pride vs. Humility

Pride says, "I can do it! I can get myself out of this mess without God or anyone else's help."

• Why is pride a killer?

• Explain what is meant by the statement, "Humility is confidence properly placed."

• Begin Step 5 by expressing your commitment to live humbly before God. Let the prayer below guide you:

Dear heavenly Father, You have said that pride goes before destruction and an arrogant spirit before stumbling. I confess that I have been thinking mainly of myself and not of others. I have not denied myself, picked up my cross daily, and followed You. I have believed that I am the only one who cares about me, so I must take care of myself. I have turned away from You and have not let You love me.

I am tired of living for myself and by myself. I now confess that I have sinned against You by placing my will before Yours and by centering my life around myself instead of You. I renounce my pride and selfishness. I cancel any ground gained by the enemies of the Lord Jesus Christ.

I ask You to fill me with Your Holy Spirit so I can do Your will. I give my heart to You and stand against all the ways that Satan attacks me. I ask You to show me how to live for others. I now choose to make other people more important than myself and to make You the most important of all. I ask this in the name of Christ Jesus my Lord, amen.

(SEE PROVERBS 16:18; MATTHEW 16:24; ROMANS 12:10)

- Now allow God to show you any specific areas in your life where you have been prideful. God can use the list on page 218 in the text to prompt you.

    —For each statement on page 218 in the text that is true for you, pray this aloud:

    Lord, I agree that I have been prideful in the area of_____. Please forgive me for my pride. I choose to humble myself and place all my confidence in You. In Jesus' name, amen.

Dealing with Prejudice and Bigotry

Pride sets one person or group against another. Satan's strategy is always to divide and conquer, but God has given us the work of reconciliation.

- How does our position in Christ wipe out any cause or motive for prejudice and bigotry?

- Look at your own heart as you ask God to show you areas of proud prejudice:

  > *Dear heavenly Father, I know that You love all people equally and that You do not play favorites. You accept people from every nation who fear You and do what is right. You do not judge them based on skin color, race, how much money they have, ethnic background, gender, what church they go to, or any other worldly matter.*
  >
  > *I confess that I have too often prejudged others or thought of myself as superior because of these things. I have not always been a minister of reconciliation, but have promoted division through my attitudes, words, and deeds. I repent of all hateful bigotry and proud prejudice, and I ask You, Lord, to now show to my mind all the ways this kind of pride has polluted my heart and mind. In Jesus' name, amen.*

- For each area of prejudice, superiority, or bigotry that the Lord brings to your mind, pray the following prayer out loud from your heart:

  > *I confess and renounce the prideful sin of prejudice against (<u>name the group</u>). I thank You for Your forgiveness, Lord, and ask now that You would change my heart and make me a loving agent of reconciliation with (<u>name the group</u>). In Jesus' name, amen.*

When we are prideful, we place our will before God's and center our life on ourselves instead of God. When we humbly acknowledge who God is, we once again acknowledge that He is our life and our source of life.

Step 6: Bondage vs. Freedom

This step to freedom deals with sins that have become habits.

- Have any sins in your life become habits? The answer may be yes if you feel caught in the trap of sin-confess-sin-confess.

- James 5:16 tells us to confess our sins to one another. What spiritually mature person will you confess to and then ask to hold you up in prayer and check in on you from time to time?

- Rewrite the promise of 1 John 1:9, using the words "I," "my," and "me." After all, this promise is for you!

- Whether you need to confess to others or just to God, pray the prayer below to begin Step 6:

> Dear heavenly Father, You have said, "Put on the Lord Jesus Christ, and make no provision for the flesh in regard to its lusts" [Romans 13:14]. I understand that I have given in to fleshly lusts, which wage war against my soul. I thank You that in Christ my sins are forgiven, but I have broken Your holy law and given the enemy an opportunity to wage war in my body.

> *I come before Your presence to admit these sins
> and to seek Your cleansing so that I may be freed
> from the bondage of sin. I now ask You to reveal to
> my mind the ways that I have broken Your moral
> law and disappointed the Holy Spirit. In Jesus'
> precious name I pray, amen.*
>
> (See 1 Peter 2:11; Romans 6:12,13;
> James 4:1; 1 Peter 5:8; 1 John 1:9)

There are many sins of the flesh that can control us. Galatians 5:19-21, Ephesians 4:25-31, and Mark 7:20-23 can help us identify these so we can give them up and turn to God and His truth in our lives.

- Ask the Lord to reveal each way you have sinned, using the checklist on page 222 to make as complete a record as possible of those things you need to confess.

- Confess each of these sins specifically by praying:

> *Lord, I confess that I have committed the sin of
> (name the sin). Thank You for Your forgiveness
> and cleansing. I now turn away from this sin and
> turn to You, Lord. Strengthen me by Your Holy
> Spirit to obey You. In Jesus' name, amen.*

Wrong Sexual Uses of Our Body

It is our responsibility to not allow sin to have control over our bodies. We must not use our bodies or another person's body as an instrument of unrighteousness (Romans 6:12,13).

- If you are struggling with habitual sexual sins, pray this prayer:

> *Lord, I ask You to bring to my mind every sexual
> use of my body as an instrument of unrighteous-
> ness so I can renounce these sins right now. In
> Jesus' name I pray, amen.*

- As the Lord brings to your mind every wrong sexual use of your body, whether it was done to you (rape, incest, sexual molestation) or willingly by you (pornography, masturbation, sexual promiscuity, petting), renounce *every* occasion:

> *Lord, I renounce (<u>name the specific use of your body</u>) with (<u>name any other person involved</u>), and I renounce any bonding that may have taken place.*

- After you are finished, commit your body to the Lord by praying:

> *Lord, I renounce all these uses of my body as an instrument of unrighteousness, and I confess any willful participation. I now present my whole body to You as a living sacrifice, holy and acceptable to You, and I reserve the sexual use of my body for only the way You intended.*
>
> *I renounce the lie of Satan that my body is not clean, that it is dirty or in any way unacceptable as a result of my past sexual experiences. Lord, I thank You that You have totally cleansed and forgiven me, that You love and accept me unconditionally. Therefore, I can accept myself. And I choose to do so, to accept myself and my body as cleansed. In Jesus' name, amen.*

Special Prayers for Special Needs

- If the Lord has brought to your mind a special need, use one of these prayers to confess your sin, renounce deception, and claim your freedom in Christ in that area.

Homosexuality

Lord, I renounce the lie that You have created me or anyone else to be homosexual, and I agree that You clearly forbid homosexual behavior. I accept myself as a child of God and declare that You created me a man (or woman). I renounce any bondages of

Satan that have perverted my relationships with others. I announce that I am free to relate to the opposite sex in the way You intended. In Jesus' name, amen.

Abortion
Lord, I confess that I was not a proper guardian and keeper of the life You entrusted to me, and I ask Your forgiveness. I choose to accept Your forgiveness by forgiving myself, and I now commit that child to You for Your care in eternity. In Jesus' name, amen.

Suicidal Tendencies
I renounce the lie that I can find peace and freedom by taking my own life. Satan is a thief, and he comes to steal, kill, and destroy. I choose life in Christ, who said He came to give me life and to give it abundantly.

Eating Disorders or Self-Mutilation
I renounce the lie that my value as a person is dependent on how I look on the outside. I renounce cutting or abusing myself, vomiting, starving myself, or using laxatives as a means of cleansing myself of evil, and I announce that only the blood of the Lord Jesus Christ can cleanse me from my sin.

I accept the reality that there may be sin present in me because of the lies I have believed and the wrongful use of my body, but I renounce the lie that I am evil or that any part of my body is evil. I announce the truth that I am totally accepted by Christ, just as I am.

Substance Abuse
Lord, I confess that I have misused substances (alcohol, tobacco, food, prescription or street drugs) for the purpose of pleasure, to escape reality, or to

cope with difficult problems. I confess that I have abused my body and programmed my mind in a harmful way. I have not allowed Your Holy Spirit to guide me.

I ask Your forgiveness, and I renounce any satanic connection or influence in my life through my misuse of drugs. I cast my cares onto Christ who loves me, and I commit myself to no longer give in to substance abuse but to follow the Holy Spirit's leading. I ask You, heavenly Father, to fill me with Your Holy Spirit. In Jesus' name, amen.

• After you have confessed all the sin you are aware of, close with this prayer:

Dear Father, I now confess these sins to You and claim, through the blood of the Lord Jesus Christ, my forgiveness and cleansing. I cancel all ground that evil spirits have gained through my willful involvement in sin. I ask this in the wonderful name of my Lord and Savior Jesus Christ, amen.

When you confess your sin, God gives you the assurance through His Holy Spirit that you have been forgiven and cleansed. In His power, you are free from the bondage of sin. In His strength, you can walk according to the Spirit and not according to the flesh.

Step 7: Curses vs. Blessings

The next step to freedom is to renounce the sins of your ancestors as well as any curses that may have been placed on you by deceived and evil people or groups.

• Iniquities can be passed down to us from previous generations if we don't renounce the sins of our ancestors and claim our new spiritual heritage in Christ.

— As far as you know, have any of your ancestors done anything that might make you vulnerable to Satan's attack?

— What three things can cause you to struggle with a particular sin?

• Ask the Lord to show you specifically what sins are characteristic of your family by praying the following prayer:

> *Dear heavenly Father, I ask You to reveal to me now all the sins of my ancestors that are being passed down through family lines. I want to be free from those influences and walk in my new identity as a child of God. In Jesus' name, amen.*

• As the Lord brings these areas of family sin to your mind, list them on a separate sheet of paper if you haven't already written them down on pages 227–228 of the text.

• In order to walk free from the sins of your ancestors and any curses and assignments targeted against you, read the following declaration and pray the following prayer out loud.

Declaration
I here and now reject and disown all the sins of my ancestors. I specifically renounce the sins of (<u>list here the areas of family sin the Lord revealed to you</u>).
As one who has now been delivered from the domain of darkness into the kingdom of God's Son,

I cancel out all demonic working that has been passed down to me from my family. As one who has been crucified and raised with Jesus Christ and who sits with Him in heavenly places, I renounce all satanic assignments that are directed toward me and my ministry. I cancel out every curse that Satan and his workers have put on me. I announce to Satan and all his forces that Christ became a curse for me when He died for my sins on the cross.

I reject any and every way in which Satan may claim ownership of me. I belong to the Lord Jesus Christ, who purchased me with His own blood. I reject all blood sacrifices whereby Satan may claim ownership of me. I declare myself to be fully and eternally signed over and committed to the Lord Jesus Christ.

By the authority I have in Christ, I now command every enemy of the Lord Jesus that is influencing me to leave my presence. I commit myself to my heavenly Father to do His will from this day forward.

(See Galatians 3:13)

Prayer

Dear heavenly Father, I come to You as Your child, bought out of slavery to sin by the blood of the Lord Jesus Christ. You are the Lord of the universe and the Lord of my life. I submit my body to You as an instrument of righteousness, a living and holy sacrifice, so I may glorify You in my body. I now ask You to fill me with the Holy Spirit. I commit myself to the renewing of my mind in order to prove that Your will is good, acceptable, and perfect for me. All this I pray in the name and authority of the risen Lord Jesus Christ, amen.

Remember, you have all the authority and protection you need in Christ to claim and keep your freedom!

Maintaining Your Freedom

Once you have secured your freedom by going through these seven steps, you may find demonic influences attempting reentry days or even months later.

- Who must we depend on for our freedom?

- What will you do to remain in right relationship with God and free of Satan's hold? Be specific.

When we call upon Jesus, the highest authority in heaven and earth, He escorts the enemy out of our lives. But it's our responsibility not to let him back in. We must hold on to the truth of our identity in Christ, stand firm, and resist the evil one.

A Step Toward Freedom

- Read Galatians 5:1. What does this promise mean to you personally? Memorize this verse and cling to its truth whenever demonic influences attempt to enter or reenter your life.

- As you pray, thank God for the freedom available in Him. Thank Him, too, for His love for you, a love that will never let you go. Then ask your all-knowing and almighty Father to show you what in your life may be keeping you from living free in Christ...and to give you the strength you need as you battle Satan and his demons. Close with a prayer of commitment. Let God know of your determination to continue to grow in Him and walk in the freedom He offers you.

Living Free and Staying Free

FOURTEEN

The freedom you gained by working through the Steps to Freedom in Chapter 13 must be maintained. You have won a very important battle, but the war goes on. Freedom is yours as long as you keep choosing truth and standing firm in the strength of the Lord. So now we'll look at seven important Bible-based guidelines to help you maintain your freedom and walk in Christ.

Remember that you don't get any extra points with God if you follow these seven guidelines. Neither do you lose points with Him if you ignore them. God loves you whether you follow His guidelines or not. However, His strong desire is that you choose to follow Him and walk in the freedom He has given you through the sacrificial death of His Son, your Savior, Jesus Christ.

1. Strengthen Your Freedom with Fellowship

God never intended that we live the Christian life alone. That's why He created the church.

- In Hebrews 10:25 and 3:13, what are believers called to do?

- What can happen when we worship, pray, and study God's Word together? What has happened to you and your walk of faith when you have done so? And what has happened when you haven't?

- How has having good friends who are brothers and sisters in the Lord helped you in your walk of faith? Or how could such friends help you?

- How are you involved in your church? Is God urging you to get more plugged in to your youth group? What will you do in response to this?

If we avoid going to church and meeting with other Christians, we become weak and vulnerable to the enemy's attacks. But when we worship, pray, and study God's Word together, we are able to build one another up in our faith.

2. Strengthen Your Freedom by Studying God's Word

The primary way to get to know God is to get to know His Word, the Bible. Reading God's Word, studying it, and memorizing key verses will help guarantee that you'll experience your freedom in Christ.

- According to Ezra 7:10, what is one reason why Ezra was greatly used by God?

- Evaluate your Bible study or quiet time.
  — What could you do to be more faithful?

  — What time is best for you to read and study the Bible? What place is best for you? What format is best for you?

  — Who can you go to for guidance and direction?

  — What is the first step you'll take to improve your Bible study time?

In 2 Timothy 2:15, you are instructed to "be diligent to present yourself approved to God as a workman who does not need to be ashamed, handling accurately the word of truth." What a great way to live free!

3. Strengthen Your Freedom Through Daily Prayer

Proverbs 15:8 tells us that God "delights in the prayers of his people" (TLB). And because of the relationship we have with God that Christ's death, burial, and resurrection made possible, we are free to go before God on our own whenever we want to.

- Do you talk to God about anything and everything? What areas of your life do you hesitate to bring before Him?

- Do you talk to God anytime and anywhere? What keeps you from staying in touch with Him throughout the course of your day?

- Review the three sample prayers found on pages 236–238 in the text.
  — What did you learn about prayer from these examples?

  — Which lines will you make a regular part of your own prayers?

Commit yourself to talk to God every day, not just during your quiet time but anytime.

4. Strengthen Your Freedom by Taking Every Thought Captive

If you want to stay free in Christ, you must assume responsibility for your thought life. Taking every thought captive to the obedience of Christ (2 Corinthians 10:5), you must reject the lies, choose the truth, and stand firm in your position in Christ.

- What is God calling you to do through Philippians 4:8,9? Be specific.

- What aspect of taking every thought captive do you most struggle with?

- What will you do about the struggle(s) you just identified? Who will you talk to about your struggle and, in turn, receive encouragement and prayer from?

Remember, you are not trying to dispel the darkness. You are turning on the light, and you do so by choosing the truth whenever a lie comes your way.

5. Strengthen Your Freedom by Understanding Who You Are in Christ

You will grow in freedom as you continue to better understand and more fully accept your identity and worth in Christ. And you can do that by filling your mind with the truth from God's Word about the acceptance, security, and significance that are yours in Christ.

- Read aloud the affirmations listed under "Who Am I?" (pages 239–242 in the text). Write out the two or three truths that give you the strength you need today. Memorize them, as well as the verses they are based on.

- Now read aloud the affirmations listed under "Since I am in Christ, by the grace of God..." (pages 242–244). Again, write out the two or three truths which are most meaningful to you today. After you've memorized your "Who Am I?" statements and verses, memorize these.

- What can you learn about yourself from the "Who Am I?" and "Since I am in Christ, by the grace of God..." lists? How did you feel about yourself after reading about who you are in Christ? What do you understand more clearly as a result of reading these statements? What do you better understand about your ability to be free from Satan and his demons?

Turn to the "Who Am I?" and "Since I am in Christ" statements—especially the ones you are memorizing—whenever you are involved in spiritual conflict. Let these truths about your scriptural identity and position in Christ form the foundation of your freedom in Him.

6. Strengthen Your Freedom Through Sharing Your Faith

As one of God's children, you have the privilege and responsibility of telling others how you came to know Jesus as your Savior and how you came to experience your freedom in Christ.

- How are you and the Holy Spirit partners when it comes to sharing your faith? What is your job and what is His?

- Which non-Christian friends can you be praying for? Make a list—and pray!

- Which Christian friends aren't experiencing freedom in Christ? Add their names to your prayer list.

- How do you feel when you think about sharing your faith? Are those feelings from God or from Satan? What will you do with them?

Sharing your faith is simply going to other people in the power of the Holy Spirit and confidently talking with them about the truths of the Bible. It's telling them how you came to know Christ and found your freedom in Him.

7. Strengthen Your Freedom by Seeking Forgiveness from Others

Since humility is one of the characteristics of our new identity in Christ, humbly asking for forgiveness will help reinforce who we are.

- Who or what is it that helps us remember the wrongs we have done to others?

- How do we decide whether our wrongs require us to go to another person to ask forgiveness?

- As God brings to your mind those people whose forgiveness you need to ask for, use the step-by-step process on pages 247–248 in the text to direct you.

Making things right with other people will help you experience your freedom in Christ more and more!

A Final Step Toward Freedom

We hope that, through this book and this study guide, you have come to know Jesus Christ better.

- Read Hebrews 10:23-25. What instruction do you find here? What encouragement for the life of freedom do you find in these verses?

- Thank God for sending His Son to be your Bondage Breaker....Thank Him for His written Word that presents the truth of Christ...and His Spirit who guides you into all truth. Thank God for what you have learned in this book....

  Then share with God your concerns about your walk of faith. Acknowledge the areas of vulnerability you are aware of. Ask Him to give you confidence in Him during your battles against Satan and his demons....

  Close with thanksgiving and praise for your Savior and Bondage Breaker...and let your words encourage you in your walk of faith. After all, God has given you all you need to win the battle for your mind, to walk in freedom, and live your life in Christ.

Remember that Jesus Christ is the Bondage Breaker and that through Him you have been set free—free to be yourself and free to grow in Him. He will always be there for you so that you can stay free in Him.

God has said, "Never will I leave you; never will I forsake you."
...Jesus Christ is the same yesterday and today and forever.
—HEBREWS 13:5,8 NIV

In...Christ Himself...are hidden all the treasures
of wisdom and knowledge.
—COLOSSIANS 2:2,3

The Bondage Breaker Youth Edition
by Neil Anderson and Dave Park

Stomping Out the Darkness
by Neil Anderson and Dave Park

Stomping Out the Darkness Study Guide
by Neil Anderson and Dave Park

Busting Free Youth Curriculum
by Dave Park

Busting Free Video Series
by Dave Park

FREEDOM IN CHRIST 4 TEENS
Higher Ground
by Neil Anderson, Robert Saucy, and Dave Park

Purity Under Pressure
by Neil Anderson and Dave Park

DEVOTIONAL SERIES
Extreme Faith
by Neil Anderson and Dave Park

Reality Check
by Neil Anderson and Rich Miller

Awesome God
by Neil Anderson and Rich Miller

Ultimate Love
by Neil Anderson and Dave Park

Righteous Pursuit
by Neil Anderson and Dave Park

Real Life
by Neil Anderson and Dave Park

Freedom
in Christ Youth Ministries
presents...

Stomping Out the Darkness
Youth Conferences

These conferences are held nationwide and are designed to help young people understand their identity in Christ and the battle for the mind. Topics that are covered include:

- Who Are You?
- Faith Renewal
- Strongholds and the Renewing of Our Minds
- Healing Damaged Emotions
- Getting Along with Others
- Forgiving from the Heart
- The Position, Authority, and Protection of the Believer

Freedom in Christ Ministries also hosts Youth Worker Training seminars for individuals who are involved in youth counseling.

For more information about Freedom in Christ Youth Ministries and their resources, or to find out current conference locations and dates, call or write:

Freedom in Christ Ministries
16071 W. Sherman St.
Goodyear, AZ 85338
Voice: 623-925-5555
Fax: 623-925-1234
E-mail: davepark@integrity.com
Website: www.ficyouth.com